no pet left behind

no pet left behind

The Sherpa® Guide to Traveling with Your Best Friend

Gayle Martz with Delilah Smittle

THOMAS NELSON
Since 1798

NASHVILLE   DALLAS   MEXICO CITY   RIO DE JANEIRO   BEIJING

Published in Nashville, Tennessee, by Thomas Nelson. Thomas Nelson is a registered trademark of Thomas Nelson, Inc.

Thomas Nelson, Inc., titles may be purchased in bulk for educational, business, fund-raising, or sales promotional use. For information, please e-mail SpecialMarkets@ThomasNelson.com.

Sherpa® is a registered trademark of Sherpa's Pet Trading Company® and is used by permission.

Library of Congress Cataloging-in-Publication Data

Martz, Gayle.
  No pet left behind : the Sherpa guide to traveling with your best friend / Gayle Martz, with Delilah Smittle.
      p. cm.
  Includes bibliographical references and index.
  978-1-4016-0344-1
  I. Pets and travel. I. Smittle, Delilah. II. Title.
  SF415.45.M37 2008
  636.088'7—dc22

                                2007041996

Printed in the United States of America
08 09 10 11 12 13 RRD 5 4 3

A LifeTime Media Production
LifeTime Media, Inc.
352 Seventh Avenue
New York, NY 10001
www.lifetimemedia.com

Editor: Karyn Gerhard
Illustrator: Dee Densmore D'Amico
Designer: Roger Gorman

contents

Preface 6

Introduction 10

part I

ready, set...

chapter 1:   Things to Remember 16

chapter 2:   Train Your Pet 30

chapter 3:   Pet Etiquette 46

chapter 4:   The Things Pets Do 58

part II

...go!

chapter 5:   Domestic Travel 72

chapter 6:   International Travel 98

chapter 7:   The Best Places to Travel with Your Pet 122

chapter 8:   If Your Pet Gets Lost or Sick 152

Resources 162

Checklists 208

Acknowledgments 212

Index 214

About the Authors 224

a tail of love and commitment

I love my pets, and I love to travel. And I cannot imagine having to choose between the two. Globetrotting with my pets has become my way of life, but not so long ago, things were very different.

In 1987, Sherpa, an adorable gray Lhasa Apso given to me by my fiancé, became my everything when my fiancé tragically died in his sleep a month before our wedding. Without a signed will, I wasn't entitled to any of his estate and had to leave our New York home. To make matters worse, after two decades as a flight attendant, I had recently been laid off during a strike. At thirty-seven years old, my entire world had been turned upside down.

Feeling alone and distraught, I wanted to spend some time with my mother, who lived in California, but I hesitated because the only way that Sherpa could accompany me on the plane was in a small hard-sided pet carrier that would be uncomfortable for her and cumbersome for me. I finally decided to leave her with a friend.

After arriving in California, I was appalled to learn that my friend's husband had placed Sherpa in a kennel. (Kennels then were not what they are now.) But worse than that, I felt completely lost without my little best friend; I realized I was the victim of a travel industry that had caused me to separate from my pooch during the time I needed her most.

At that moment, a new commitment was born. I vowed to devote

my energy to broadening the industry's pet-in-cabin policy to accept an alternative to the hard-sided carrier. My diverse international travel experiences, coupled with the time I had spent as an aspiring professional photographer in the handbag industry, laid the groundwork for an idea that would revolutionize pet travel: The Sherpa Bag® — a soft-sided pet carrier.

I designed and developed my first The Sherpa Bag® with my Sherpa's comfort and ease of travel in mind. It provided proper ventilation to keep her comfortable, had plenty of pockets for water bottles and toys, included a detachable leash, and most important, fit perfectly under an airline seat. That pet carrier encouraged those airlines that did not accept small pets in the passenger cabin to change their pet-in-cabin policies. I lobbied the airlines myself, one by one. American and TWA were among the first to officially approve The Sherpa Bag® for onboard use, and others soon followed. My Sherpa Bag® became the first officially approved in-cabin soft-sided pet carrier.

I had little business experience and absolutely no financing. I borrowed five thousand dollars from my mother to have the bags made and then pounded the pavement, selling them from store to store on my own. I targeted the stores I knew — Bloomingdales, Saks, Macys, and Hammacher Schlemmer. I designed the bags, distributed and shipped them, and handled the business from my 800 number. In the process, I spread awareness about traveling with pets. During that difficult but exhilarating time, my satisfied customers made it all worthwhile — and helped me spread the word about this revolutionary approach to pet travel!

By 1994, The Sherpa Bag® was officially approved by ten airlines. Today, The Sherpa® Trading Company manufactures more than a hundred different bags, collars, leashes, pet throws, and car seat covers that are sold in the United States, Canada, Europe, and Japan.

Life is all about change, and just a few years ago, another major change took place in my world. My beloved Lhasa Apso, Sherpa, the namesake of my company and my companion for seventeen years, passed away. Though I miss her still, her spirit lives on. When Sherpa was ten years old, I adopted SuNae, my gorgeous Coton du Tulear, whose Korean name means "true love." SuNae was originally named Sweetie Pie, but as soon as I met her, I knew a name change was in order. She was to be groomed as Sherpa's protégé, and "Sweetie Pie" just didn't fit. (Although she is a sweetie pie!)

SuNae is a strong-willed little girl and a source of comfort, inspiration, and friendship to me. I also just adopted a young Shih Tzu whom I named Kartu. Though SuNae is not exactly thrilled about having to share me with Kartu, I'm certain that she'll soon learn to enjoy Kartu's friendship, just as Sherpa enjoyed SuNae's.

Pets make a huge difference in our lives, and it is up to us as pet lovers to ensure that our pets are not left behind. We haven't yet reached a point in our society where pets are accepted everywhere and treated as the family members that they are. But we do not have to live with unfair laws and regulations; we can work together toward change and acceptance.

My reason for writing this book is to share my knowledge and experience concerning pet travel. I wanted to create a kind of pet travel "bible"—a reliable source that people can trust and turn to when they have questions and concerns, or just want to learn how to travel with a pet.

Note to readers: Throughout the book I make many references to Sherpa®-branded products because, in addition to being the market leader for pet travel gear, the Sherpa® brand is near and dear to my heart. Though I reference the Sherpa® brand, there are other brands of pet travel gear that are suitable for traveling with your pet. When making your selections, choose a product that best fits the needs of you and your pet.

Who unfailingly loves your cooking, puts pep in your step, a smile on your face, and a song in your heart? Whether it's a cold, wet nose, a whisper of fur brushing against your ankle, or a chirp or whistle that greets you at day's end, your most steadfast admirer is also your best friend: your pet. But even though he's always there for you, your constant cheerleader can become bored with his daily routine, be it life in the not-so-great indoors, a quick game of Frisbee in the backyard, or a leashed walk around the neighborhood.

Life is so much richer when you take your pet with you on your outings—from the fun places you can explore together to your must-do errands. Pets naturally enjoy the great outdoors, so why not take them out and about as often as possible? The next time you meet your friends for lunch or happy hour, go alfresco—meet them at a sidewalk café and take your best buddy along. Tuck your "pocket" pet (cats, ferrets, and small dogs) into a stylish, go-anywhere pet tote, and share a spontaneous window-shopping excursion through a trendy shopping district or a relaxing, sunset walk on the beach. Or get out the leash and take your buddy of the larger canine persuasion to a dog park, activity-filled doggie day camps sponsored by a local pet shop, or on a hiking and camping excursion. You may find yourself exploring new-to-you activities as you strategize your pet-inspired day trips, weekend getaways, and even vacations to far-flung island destinations or foreign countries.

No matter what the species, our pets are part of our family and we want to take them along on vacations—don't think that if your pet is not a dog, you'll have to put your travel plans on hold. A

well-behaved pet, no matter what the species, is accepted many places—the amazing assortment of certified therapy pets out there bears this out. I've even met a pair of guinea pigs and a snake that accompany their owner to children's story hours and nursing homes. Cats are usually welcome anywhere dogs can go—cats have the advantage of being beautifully lightweight, portable, and quiet. If you start traveling with a kitten or cat as soon as you adopt him, he will accept travel as a normal facet of life with you and look forward to his shared outings.

Even your feathered friends can enjoy a day out! If you have a parrot, cockatiel, parakeet, or any of the parrot family members, you know just how faithful and affectionate they are. They enjoy sitting on your shoulder, looking lovingly into your eyes, and "preening" tendrils of your hair. Since these larger birds usually prefer walking to flying—and, yes, they usually prefer sitting on your shoulder to walking—they are easy to take with you and can even be trained to wear a halter and leash for safety's sake. Ask people who own cold-blooded pets like lizards and iguanas, and they will testify to their pets' intelligence and affection, and when their needs for warmth are met, these animals make quiet and curious traveling companions.

Some pet owners shy away from taking their animals on trips because of certain myths of pet travel that simply aren't true anymore. As more pets take to the road and to the air, motels and hotels are becoming increasingly pet friendly, with some actually offering pet perks such as complimentary water bowls, blankets, and even room service to lure pet-owning travelers to their establishments. These days, large roadside rest areas have dog walking areas, and some even have fenced-in dog parks. Most airlines accept pet passengers, and those pets small enough to fit in an under-the-seat carrier can travel in the cabin with you. Pet travel has become so commonplace that many airports even have dog-walking areas.

This guide is destined to become the busiest book on your shelf. In fact, it may never make it to the shelf. You may even want to have two copies—one to pack in your suitcase and one to keep in the house to help you as you plan your trips. But before hitting the road, be sure to tuck one copy into a pocket of your pet carrier, and refer to it to solve the many sudden pet situations, from easing the symptoms of motion sickness to soothing separation anxiety, that pop up while traveling with your pet.

In this book you will also discover a wealth of pet-friendly solutions, destinations, hotels, and airlines; unravel the mysteries of taxi, subway, and bus travel; find out what vaccinations, medical papers, and government permits your pet will need for traveling abroad; get the scoop on how to create a customized first-aid kit for your pet; learn what carryout and convenience-store foods make good emergency substitutes for pet food; and more.

So, read this book, enjoy, and take all the surprises out of adventuring with your pet—except the good ones!

part 1

ready,

set...

chapter 1

things
to
rem

My travel journal

My Vet: ～～～～～～

Vet in Paris: ～～～～～

Hotel: ～～～～～～

car service: ～～～

packing check list:

✓ first aid kit

✓ FOOD

✓ tREATS

ember

Prepare the Basics

Before taking off on a travel adventure with your pet, you have some preparations to complete. This chapter will let you de-stress and focus on the fun of traveling with your pet by helping you collect and organize all of your pet's "travelbilia"—from paperwork, food, and medications to carriers, beds, and toys—ahead of time.

Necessary Details

Because some travel regulations require a medical certificate issued within ten days of travel, the first priority is to take your pet to your vet for a medical examination. Make sure that your pet gets all of his shots and that the vet gives you a recent certificate of health geared to where you are traveling. In addition to collecting pet-maintenance supplies and vet records, you should review which pet papers are specifically required where you are headed and what the travel regulations are if you plan to take your pet across state and country lines. Visit www.aphis.usda.gov/ac for government pet travel rules within the United States. For more interstate and international pet travel information, see resources, pages 190, 198.

Make a Loss-Prevention Kit

Every pet should have a basic care and identification kit in case of loss or the necessity of others caring for her. Make copies of important papers and care instructions, enclose them in a clear plastic zip-close bag, and attach that to your pet's crate. If you have one of my Sherpa Bag® soft-sided carriers, you can tuck them into the zip-close side pocket. If you have a hard-sided carrier, run a border of clear packing tape around the sides of the plastic bag to attach it securely. For hard-sided crates that have a tape-resistant slick finish, abrade the area with fine sandpaper, wipe clean, and then apply tape. Inside the bag include:

Identification Papers:

- Copies of pedigree, license, health certificate, medical, and vaccination records, especially for a current rabies shot
- Contact information for your pet's vet, kennel, and breeder
- Your cell phone number and another emergency contact's phone number
- Photos of your pet labeled with his name

Pet Identification

Most of us never expect to lose our pet or to be directly affected by a natural disaster. But the unexpected does happen, and statistics show that many owners are caught by surprise and are unprepared. Identification tags are useful, and I recommend putting them on collars, leashes, and carriers. I also recommend that you fasten a duplicate set of pet tags to a halter before taking a trip and that you keep the halter on your pet at all times.

Permanent Pet ID

Although identification tags are important, in order to ensure that your pet will be returned to you if he is lost, it is best to have him marked with some form of permanent identification. There are two types of permanent pet identification:

Pet tattoos have for some time been effective in locating lost pets. An identification number is tattooed in legible numbers on the smooth skin of your pet's inner thigh. If the animal is found and reported to a vet or shelter, their office can look up the number and obtain contact information for the owner. The tattoo is constant, but the contact information can be updated as needed. Because of the large area of bare skin required, this type if identification is most suited to larger mammals, such as dogs and cats.

The microchip revolutionized the way owners protect their pets. The chip is inserted under the skin between the shoulder blades. Each chip is encoded with a unique and unalterable identification code that can be activated only when read by a scanner, and each chip has an antimigration cap that helps prevent movement of the chip within your pet's body. Most vets can inject a pet with a microchip during a routine exam.

A not-for-profit organization called Companion Animal Recovery (CAR) was founded in June 1995 by the American Kennel Club (AKC) and is dedicated to providing lifetime recovery services for animals that have been inserted with a microchip. After a pet has had a microchip inserted, the ID number is enrolled with CAR, which maintains a worldwide enrollment database and a recovery service that works 24/7 all year long. The AKC recommends the HomeAgain® microchip, which is marketed by the Schering-Plough Animal Health Corporation.

Shelters, rescue organizations, animal control officers, and veterinarians use scanners to identify lost pets. When a pet is found, CAR is contacted. Phone calls, fax, and e-mail technology go into fast action to notify the owner. As an incentive, many municipalities issue a lifetime license with a one-time charge to owners of microchipped pets. For more information, see resources, page 201.

The beauty of this system is that pets of most species (not just large mammals) can have a microchip inserted and be enrolled in CAR, and as with tattoos, your contact information can be easily changed or updated as needed.

Unique ID Tags to Make or Order

With a little ingenuity, and little or no cost, you can create temporary tags that will let anyone who finds your pet know where to return him. If you are staying at a hotel or campground, fasten its business card to your pet's collar by wrapping a strip of strong, waterproof clear tape around the collar and the card. If no paperwork is handy, write out your contact information by hand and tape it to your pet's collar.

You can make your own tags at a tag-making vending machine, which you'll find at many pet-shop franchises. These tags are big enough for three or more lines of type (include your cell phone number and address where you are staying). It is also a good idea to create one of these tags to alert people to any chronic diseases or problems.

An online service also offers ready-made pet Medical Alert Tags that are listed with the National Pet Health Registry. You can choose stainless steel tags with labels such as "seizures" or "blind," and each is engraved with a unique ID number. The ID number, including your pet's medical and veterinarian information and your pet's photo, is registered in PetHealthAlert.com's National Pet Health Registry. Download a free tag order form online (www.pethealthalert.com) or request a free tag order form by mailing a self-addressed stamped envelope to Pet Protect PetHealthAlert, P.O. Box 11447, Naples, FL 34101.

Label the Crate

Ensure that your pet's travel bag has identification tags labeled with contact telephone numbers (cell numbers are recommended). You may also want to include either the number of a friend or relative who lives outside your area, or phone numbers and contact information for your destination. I also recommend adding a tag that has your pet's picture and name.

If you have a large dog or exotic pet that must travel in a hard-sided crate, you can help attendants keep an eye on your pet's crate by personalizing it with colorful spray paint. Painting the pet's name on the crate in large letters will invite attendants to say hello and reassure your pet by using his name. You can also stencil on designs and signs. For example, stencil "Do Not Open Without Owner's Permission" to help protect against loss.

If you are short on time (or not a great painter), shop the Web or your local pet store for easy-to-read, airline-approved pet-crate identification signs, rescue signs, and decals. For around $10, these plastic signs come in a kit, along with airline-approved forms for emergency information and care and feeding instructions, and even food and water dishes that fasten to crate doors. When shopping, don't overlook "rescue" signs designed for home windows. Post one of these in a hotel room, car, or RV window to alert those who enter in an emergency that there is a pet on board.

In addition to a carrier for each pet, make sure you have sturdy leashes and harnesses to ensure that your pets cannot slip loose and get lost. Leashes, collars, and pet carriers should all have identification tags. It's a good idea to invest in an extra harness and leash—I prefer harnesses for both safety and security, as they are harder for a pet to slip out of. For a list of stores and Web sites, see the resources section.

Other Helpful Travel Items

The Trappings of Travel

What about blankets, beds, bowls, and the other accoutrements of a traveling pet? When it comes to carrier or crate travel, requirements for these items can get pretty specific. To satisfy airline regulations, you must attach food and water bowls or water tubes to the door of a pet's carrier, crate, or cage, and they must be accessible without opening the door. Many carriers come without accessories, but you can find these inexpensive snap-on bowls and water tubes in any pet store. They are convenient, but have small capacity, so you may also want to take along a pet canteen for refills and to pack full-sized pet bowls to use when you reach your destination.

Blankets and beds need to be absorbent and washable; carry an extra in case one gets soiled. You can put your pet's bedding in the carrier if it meets these needs, or buy a couple of specially designed crate beds that fit your pet's carrier.

Soft Carriers and Accessories

My Sherpa's Pet Trading Company® offers a line of totes and backpacks that provide options for carrying small- to medium-sized pets, whether on foot, in a car, or on public transportation. The totes and backpacks have mesh ventilation panels, roomy zippered pockets, an inside leash ring, and they come with a washable faux lamb's fleece liner (for proper sizing, see page 28–29).

The micro-fiber backpack is a versatile carrier, with straps that adjust from a shoulder bag to a full backpack. Like other Sherpa Bag® carriers, the backpack easily fits under an airline cabin seat.

Purse-style pet totes look like luxurious shopping bags and come in a selection of tailored or feminine fabrics with matching pet ID tag and a cushioned, washable bottom pad. Mesh panels allow pets plenty of air, and locking zippers and an interior leash ring provide security. These people-friendly bags have generous handles that loop over the arm or shoulder.

Coordinating accessory pouches slide over my soft-sided carrier's handles and make a handy place to stash toys, leashes, and other pet essentials. A selection of leashes and collars made of vinyl-reinforced fabric with silver-tone hardware and keepers match all styles of my soft-sided carriers.

When it comes to car travel, Sherpa® covers your seats with a pet-proof, washable seat cover made of plush velour with a water-resistant nylon backing. The faux-fur pet throws keep pets comfortable and furniture clean at home, in a hotel, or in the car.

Carrier Considerations

While your pet's size dictates the size and type of carrier you'll need, other aspects of your pet, such as her age and personality, create special needs that you should address to ensure her comfort when traveling.

What to Pack for Common Travel Aches and Pains

Even the healthiest pet can fall victim to temporary travel illness. If your pet suffers from motion sickness, lack of appetite, allergies, or temperature extremes, be prepared. If you know that your pet is prone to travel ailments, talk to your vet about the treatments you should pack for your trip. For warm-blooded pets, such as dogs, cats, and parrots, pack soda crackers or plain oatmeal to settle their stomachs and bread to soak in water or lettuce for birds, rodents, and cold-blooded pets for a treat that will also hydrate. If your pet is sensitive to cold, pack a sweater or a blanket to cover the cage. It is also wise to carry a small spray bottle with water, as most animals and birds will cool off when spritzed with tepid water under their forelegs (the place that corresponds to your armpits). Another item to ward off the effects of heat is a bandana, which you can moisten with water and wrap around the neck of a dog or cat, if she will tolerate it. For more on travel first aid, see page 202.

Gearing Up for Various Modes of Public Transportation

According to AAA, the most popular form of travel with pets is by car, and for good reason. Most states prohibit animals from riding on buses, and similar regulations restrict travel on trains. Exceptions are made for guide and service dogs accompanying blind and disabled persons. No pets, except service animals, are permitted on Greyhound® buses or Amtrak trains in the United States. However, rules and policies change periodically, so check with Greyhound® and Amtrak before planning a trip. Local rail and bus companies may allow pets in small carriers, but this is more of an exception than common practice. Airlines accept pets on an individual carrier basis.

Be sure to check the individual carrier's rules in advance to keep your pet from being rejected or possibly confiscated. When you buy your ticket, specify the species of animal, because some may be banned. Once you determine whether the company permits your pet to travel, be sure to find out the details regarding what documentation and type of carrier or crate you need.

Whether you plan to take a short trip by car or taxi or a full-fledged vacation, you need basic equipment, including a leash, halter, and identification tags (if your pet does not wear a halter, fasten tags to the carrier or cage). Be sure to use washable bedding, pack your pet's favorite food and treats, and keep him supplied with water from home (strange drinking water can upset stomachs).

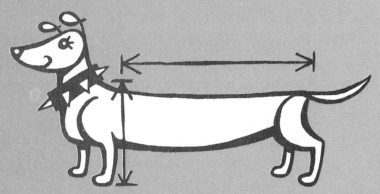

Soft-sided Sherpa Bag® pet totes are great for local jaunts but do not meet airline requirements. If your goal is to take your pet into the airline cabin, you should purchase an airline-approved soft-sided carrier. Sizing is important—your pet's carrier should provide safe and comfortable travel. For a proper fit, begin by carefully measuring and weighing your pet.

Guidelines

When measuring your pet, length refers to the area from the nape of the neck (where the collar falls) to the base of the tail. Height is measured from the floor to the shoulder. Weight is important because your pet must not exceed the maximum weight allowances for the carrier you choose.

Once you have your pet's measurements, follow the manufacturer's guidelines for choosing the correct carrier bag size. Your pet should be able to stand up and turn around when the carrier is closed (which is more than you can do in your airline seat!).

Generally, cats use the medium bag. Small carrier bags are only for the teeniest teacup dog breeds. Medium bags accommodate most small dogs weighing fewer than sixteen pounds. Large bags are suitable for animals between sixteen and twenty-two pounds. The exact fit will depend on the shape and dimensions of your pet. Remember that this carrier is a "room" for your pet and not a mobile home—do not go overboard on the size. Sherpa, my Lhasa Apso, is a helpful example. Sherpa traveled in a medium-sized bag. She was sixteen inches long from the nape of her neck to the base of her tail, was ten inches high at the shoulder, and weighed fifteen pounds.

Pet Carrier Sizing		
For Pets Up To:	Use Carrier Size:	
5 lbs	12"L x 7"H	Mini
8 lbs	13"L x 8"H	Small
16 lbs	16"L x 10"H	Medium
22 lbs	18"L x 11"H	Large

Pet Tote Sizing		
For Pets Up To:	Use Tote Size:	
10 lbs	13"L x 8"H	Small
16 lbs	16"L x 10"H	Medium

Look for a carrier bag that is durable, adequately ventilated, and made from an easy-to-clean material. Today, so many styles, colors, and designs are available that you may decide to purchase more than one bag to coordinate with what you (and your pet) are wearing or to reflect your travel destination.

If your dog is too large to fit under an airline seat, use the same measurement rules to size your dog to a hard-sided travel crate. Take your dog to the pet shop to "try on" a new carrier or crate. She should be able to stand up and turn around in it to meet airline requirements.

train
yo

Well-trained pets—so beautifully in sync with their owners—are a pleasure to observe, whether a therapy pet giving solace to a hospital patient or a companion dog calmly and confidently striding alongside his owner through the hustle and bustle of an airport. Well-trained pets are relaxed and calm; they focus on their owners and engage in ongoing communication. Training your pet offers him balance because all animal species have a pack or pecking order in nature and are most comfortable and thrive within rules and boundaries that they understand.

As lovable as an untrained pet is to its owner, he is inevitably annoying to fellow travelers, and worse, his safety and security are in jeopardy. An untrained pet is also at risk of being lost or injured if he dashes heedlessly from his carrier, a car door, or a hotel room.

In this chapter, you will learn how to familiarize your pet with travel carriers and how to recognize what types of toys, bowls, and blankets are safe choices for traveling pets. You will discover how to acclimate your pet by taking him on short "practice trips" around the neighborhood by car and public transportation, and you will also find tips for traveling with pets who may be difficult or have special needs.

Train Your Pet to Travel in a Carrier

Your pet's carrier is her home away from home. Right from the start, she needs to sense that her carrier is a safe "den"—a place where she can retreat when she needs to feel secure and protected. Whether your pet is young, old, or somewhere in between, her first experiences with the carrier should be positive and brief, so that she will look forward to seeing the carrier come out.

To help your pet accept a new carrier as her own, give it a familiar scent. Put one of her stuffed toys or his bed, along with a worn T-shirt or other garment, inside for a day or two before you introduce your pet to the carrier. Begin by allowing her to explore the carrier on her own. Once she thoroughly sniffs it, rubs against it, enters it, exits it, and perhaps, climbs on top of it, you can then begin training her to enter on command.

Tap the top of the carrier when you want her to enter. Remember that you're trying to establish a ritual because pets love rituals and routines. Repeat the tapping action until she realizes that it is her cue to go inside. When she follows your tapping command and enters, praise her and reward her with a treat, making sure that her going into the carrier is a consistently positive experience. If she is a little slow to catch on or hesitant about entering, increase her comfort level by placing a special

no pet left behind train your pet

Traveling Toys

When you're traveling you can read a book, work on your laptop, or listen to music, but what about your pet? To make sure he doesn't get bored, add a few new toys to his carrier. Favorites are "puzzle-type" toys, such as a Kong® dog toy stuffed with peanut butter and then frozen. What you stuff your pet's toy with depends on what he loves. Playing with toys engages your pet in a positive activity while traveling. But because it is difficult for you to see what he's doing with a toy while you are driving or flying, you must think safety first when selecting a travel toy.

Safe Toys

- Raw beef leg bone—a butcher can cut them in short or long pieces to suit the size of your pet's mouth (for dogs or parrots)
- Durable nylon chew toys (for dogs or parrots)
- Hollow hard rubber toys to fill with kibble or peanut butter (for dogs, cats, or parrots)
- Durable catnip toy that can't be torn apart or swallowed (for cats)
- Wad of paper suspended by a string tied to the ceiling of a carrier (for cats)
- Disposable cardboard scratching pad (for cats)
- Commercial chew sticks or cardboard toilet-paper cores (for rodents)
- Spray millet (for birds)
- Stainless steel "mirror" (for birds)

Unsafe Toys

- Soft, stuffed toys, which can be torn apart and swallowed
- Rawhide toys, which can be broken apart and swallowed (these can obstruct airways or intestines)
- Cooked bones or chicken bones, which can shatter when chewed and cause internal injury
- Glass mirrors, which can break and cause injury
- Squeaky toys, which can be torn apart and the squeaker swallowed

treat in the carrier. Do not be discouraged if she grabs the treat and runs. Just going into the carrier voluntarily is a success worth celebrating. Repeat this activity a few times, and be sure to talk to her while she is in the crate. That will help her relax and stay a little longer each time.

The routine just described works best with dogs, who readily take to training. If your cat is a bit too independent to enter the carrier on command, try this technique: Lay the carrier on its side with the door hinge at the top, so that gravity causes the door to close. Hold the door open while you set the cat inside. As you remove your hands, the weight of the door will cause it to quickly shut. Now you can latch the door and gently right the carrier.

Troubleshooting

Never strap a pet carrier in the front passenger seat of a car. The force of a deployed air bag may seriously injure a pet even if he's in a carrier. Instead, put the carrier in the back seat and strap it in securely by running the seat belt through the handle and around the side of the carrier.

Have Carrier, Will Travel

Now you can take the carrier training a step further. The next time your pet enters the carrier at your tap, instead of giving him a treat right away, close the carrier and take a "trip" to the kitchen, talking to him the whole time. Once in the kitchen, open the carrier and then give him a treat—another positive experience. After you repeat several "trips" to the kitchen and to other places in your home, your pet understands that he can "go places" in his carrier, and he associates these "trips" with praise and treats. His carrier has become a positive element in his life—a home away from home—and he feels calm and safe when in it.

Your cat may actually take to crate travel even more readily than your dog because cats are naturally interested in exploring nooks and crannies, and they enjoy curling up in boxes, dresser drawers, and travel crates. When acclimated, dogs will also like to retreat to a safe carrier "cave," and once yours accepts the carrier as his own, he may want to sleep in it even when you are not traveling.

You are now both ready to start exploring the world outside your home, without stress. If your pet fears riding in the car, take very small steps. First, let him sit in his carrier in the car without the engine running; maybe even play games with him in the car. Put a couple of his favorite toys and a blanket or pillow in the carrier. Once your pet is comfortable with this situation, turn on the engine and then take a "trip" up and down your driveway. Eventually, you can proceed around the block and then around town, and graduate to longer car trips.

Training for Travel Enjoyment and Safety

Some pets, especially cats, have a strong independent streak or an extreme fear of the unknown. Small, swift animals such as hamsters, ferrets, birds, amphibians, and lizards, instinctively hide when stressed. These pets will be most comfortable and safe left in the confines of a carrier or cage when traveling. But even crate-bound critters need a bit of training, so read on for some helpful tips.

Crate Training

You may be asking yourself whether training is really necessary when your pet will be traveling inside a carrier, after all. But believe me, it is important, and for several reasons. Although airlines and other public transportation may accept pets on board, they will not accept a crated pet that is noisy or aggressive, either in or out of the crate. Additionally, airlines require a carrier to be big enough for a pet to stand up and turn around in, and some baggage-check personnel will ask you to have your pet demonstrate this. Take heart: you can teach your pet an essential crate-training trick or two.

To teach your dog or cat to turn around in a crate, begin working outside the crate, because you will need to use both hands. Put a leash on your pet and tell him to stand. If he has not learned to stand on command, put your hand under his stomach, lift him to his feet, and tell him to stand. Hold the leash taut to keep him standing. Put a treat in your free hand, and make a closed fist. Hold your fist against his nose and move it around his body so that he will turn in a tight circle, keeping his nose pressed to your fist. Tell him "Turn," and then give him the treat and praise him. After a few practices, try the routine without the leash. When he has the hang of it, put the little guy in his crate and motion in a circle with your treat-holding hand in front of the closed door. When he turns around, praise him and give him the treat through the door grate. This interesting trick can come in very handy at home, as well as abroad. When your pet comes in from outdoors, have him turn in a circle on the doormat, to effectively wipe his feet!

Pets Don't Have to Be Little Stinkers

Of course, a toilet-trained dog will be happier in a crate than will an untrained pet subjected to soiled bedding. Learn to housebreak your pet by reading any dog-training book; in fact, most house-breaking techniques actually use a crate because dogs naturally resist soiling their dens and bedding. But whether your dog is housebroken or not, be sure to use washable bedding and take her for a long walk before crating her, to make sure that she has emptied her bladder.

If you travel with a small pet, such as a hamster, ferret, or guinea pig, make sure you pack plenty of clean bedding and change it often. Bad odor is one of two potential offenses of carrier-bound pets. If yours is a bird or other exotic animal, place a thick layer of newspapers in the cage before leaving home and pull out and dispose of soiled sheets as needed to keep the cage fresh. If you have a cat, purchase a carrier large enough to hold a bed and a small litter box, and scoop the litter at every opportunity.

Puppy Love

When traveling with a puppy, be sure to give her extra exercise before taking her on a trip in her carrier. A tired puppy is a quiet puppy! Lots of socialization before the trip is critical—for puppies of all ages. The puppy must be familiar with people, cars, other dogs, wheelchairs, moving vehicles, and other distractions. The more positive experiences your puppy, or older dog, has with these things, the more relaxed she will be during your trip.

On- and Off-Leash Training

To be a good traveler, your dog should be house-trained and able to obey basic commands. Though dog-obedience training is a bit beyond the scope of this book, you'll find many books and videos available on training, and just as many good obedience schools, including inexpensive programs sponsored by municipal park programs.

A great way to find a school in your area is to visit pet stores that admit pets. When you spot a well-behaved dog, ask his owner what school he attended. Or ask your vet to recommend a school.

Your dog does not have to learn every trick in the book to be a good traveling companion, but some training is very important. Knowing the three basic obedience commands—"heel," "sit," "stay"—will stand her in good stead. And they are easy; your dog can learn them in about a month's worth of obedience classes. Why does he need to learn this before we travel, you ask? Read on to see just how obedience training simplifies the complexities of traveling and keeps your dog safe.

Heel

A dog "at heel" walks beside her owner, usually on the owner's left side (most people are right-handed), with her head even with the heel of the owner's left foot—not charging ahead and pulling her hapless owner by the leash. Dogs that have learned to heel are not easily distracted because they focus on their owners and look at them frequently. If yours charges ahead of you, he is out of control and can create problems ranging from tangling himself around and tripping other people to running into oncoming traffic and possibly dragging you along with him. When others see that your dog heels beautifully at your side, he will automatically be met with approval from fellow travelers, airport staff, and hotel personnel.

Sit

A dog that jumps on people is not only annoying, but can actually injure a child or older person by knocking him down or scratching his legs. Teaching your dog to sit on command will not only make her welcome in public places, but could save her life. She should sit quietly in front of you in a hotel airport waiting area, at a rest stop, or at a sidewalk café.

Do not let your pet approach other people unless they express an interest in greeting and petting her. And when they do, have her sit when they pet her. Additionally, and importantly, a well-trained dog walking alongside her owner will sit automatically when the owner stops, such as at the intersection of two streets. This habit will keep your dog from rushing into traffic or lunging at passing cars.

Stay

Dogs have short attention spans, and you should not expect yours to sit or lie down on command for more than two or three minutes, but you can accomplish a lot in that length of time. Keeping in mind that you must always keep your dog on a leash when traveling, it can be difficult to load luggage into a taxi or hand a ticket to a driver if your dog is tugging on its leash or leaping about. Put your dog into a "sit" or "down" position, and tell him to "stay" while you wrestle with the necessary details. Remember to give him the "okay" command to release him as soon as you can devote your full attention to him again.

Did You Know?

In addition to basic obedience classes (after he graduates), you can enroll your dog in classes designed to train him as a therapy dog. The advantages of pet-therapy classes are many. They teach your dog advanced social skills, like calmly coping with and respecting all sorts of distractions from baby buggies and wheelchairs to people using walkers and canes. The payoffs include a special tag or vest that he can wear, which will allow him to accompany you to otherwise off-limit places, such as stores, shopping malls, and some restaurants, plus allowing him to visit nursing homes, hospitals, and hospices where he can bring cheer to deserving children and adults.

Tips for Traveling with Special-Needs Pets

Kathy Santos, a New Jersey-based dog behaviorist, trainer, and author of pet-behavior books, believes that dogs who are sound-sensitive, apprehensive, or fearful need a lot of extra time to become comfortable with the new sights and sounds they encounter when traveling. When socializing them for a trip, be sure to allow that extra time in case you run into a strong fear reaction. She advises speaking to a fearful dog (or any other pet, for that matter) in a casual, upbeat way—"Oh, Sam, you're fine!"—rather than to commiserate with him. Saying "It's okay, sweetie, I know you're afraid!" involves using a worrisome tone of voice, which only validates your pet's fear.

If you are traveling with a special-needs pet, be sure to label the crate with the disability, provide guidelines for handling the pet, and keep medications with your pet at all times. Whenever possible, stay with your pet and walk him around his new environment to acquaint him with where the furniture and his food and water bowls are located. If your dog or cat has vision problems, keep her at your side as you walk her through strange places so that she can focus on you rather than potential obstacles. If she is hearing-impaired, teach her obedience hand signals and to come by clapping or stamping your foot on the floor; she will feel the vibrations and respond.

Older Pets

Senior pets can have a variety of unique travel needs. What is a senior dog? Generally speaking, the smaller the dog, the longer it takes to age. Tufts University set the elderly limit for a small breed dog at twelve years, and larger breeds at six to eight years. In general, dogs reach "middle age" at around seven years; for cats, middle age is between eight and ten years. Cats can live twenty years and beyond and, if healthy, will not

no pet left behind train your pet

develop age-related ailments until the ends of their long lives. Parrots live even longer; but small animals, such as guinea pigs, rabbits, and cold-blooded pets, may be a senior pet at five or six years.

When your pet starts getting a little paunch and is moving a bit more slowly, you need to think carefully before you move her into your fast lane. Most older dogs have been socialized to the sights and sounds of the great outdoors and have had contact with many people and animals. Those with stable temperaments tend to adapt well to traveling. However, some older pets get set in their ways and often prefer a familiar and comfortable environment, so it is most important to bring along his water and food bowls, toys, chew items, favorite bedding—and extra sheets to cover bedding and furniture at your destination.

Many pets drink less as they age, which can lead to dehydration when traveling, and strange water may make them sick. Carry a container of water from home (or distilled water) and frequently offer your pet small amounts. They can also be set in their ways about food, so pack enough of their usual chow to last the duration of the trip.

Elderly pets naturally slow down, taking longer to stand up and walk than they once did, so schedule leisurely walks and practice patience when traveling. Senior pets commonly "heed the call" more frequently than younger animals. When traveling, make sure you stock up on doggie diapers, wee-wee pads, and cleanup supplies such as paper towels, soap, and water. If you have an older cat, place several disposable litter boxes around a hotel room so that she can find one when the urge strikes.

Elderly pets can also be hindered by ailments ranging from dental problems, arthritis, and obesity to more serious conditions like diabetes or thyroid disease. Schedule checkups with your vet every six months, and be sure to visit just before planning a trip so that you can update her condition and prescriptions and make sure she feels well enough to travel. Take a premium food and feed her twice daily to help regulate blood sugar and energy levels. Provide medications as scheduled, and watch for any signs of deterioration. Chronic pain can make any pet snappish. If this is true of yours, include a muzzle when you pack. It's a good idea to locate a vet in advance, but if you find yourself without one, any pet shop can help, and many have their own vets. For a list of conventional and holistic veterinarians, see resources on page 202.

Difficult Pets

Although lots of prior socializing with people and dogs independent of the carrier will help prevent your pet from howling or barking at loud noises, wheelchairs, kids, and other dogs, they still may fly off the handle when you are not close by. Playing "Peek-a-Boo" with human babies helps ease their separation anxiety, and it's also a useful exercise for teaching your pet to spend time peacefully alone. Begin by leaving your pet in a room or in his crate for a few minutes. If he is quiet, return and praise him. Wait for at least half an hour, and then try again, staying away for a few more minutes. Do this exercise daily until your pet is able to wait calmly for you to return for a few hours.

Traveling with a pet who has aggressive tendencies, either toward other animals or people, can be extremely difficult. Remember, if your airline or other travel carrier feels the animal is a threat, they will refuse to board him, and then your entire trip is ruined. Aggressive pets may also not adapt to a classroom full of other dogs, so personal trainers are available through most obedience schools to work one-on-one with your pet. If you are at all unsure of your pet's behavior upon confronting other pets or people, pack a muzzle, and put it on your pet when you take him into populated areas. If he must travel in the cargo area of a plane, be sure to label the crate with a sign signaling handlers to keep the crate closed at all times.

Teaching your pet good manners will not only make for smooth sailing but give you and your four-footed, finned, or feathered friend access to many places that normally have pet restrictions.

pet.
etiq

uette

When traveling with your pet on a plane or other public transit, and even by car, keep a low profile. You don't want to create a scene and disturb other passengers, rest-stop tourists, or hotel guests. It is a privilege to be able to travel with your pet—and it pays to be respectful of those around you.

Still, no matter how well-behaved your pet is, some people simply do not like animals. I've heard it said that a joyful soul can find happiness anywhere, but a complaining soul will find something wrong, even in paradise. You don't want to rile a complaining soul. When it comes to traveling with your pet, every form of travel requires a prescribed form of etiquette—petiquette®, if you will.

This chapter will help you and your pet relax and enjoy the trip by helping you plan ahead for accommodations, and rest assured that en route and after you reach your destination, your pet will always be on her best behavior.

Putting Fellow Travelers at Ease

I could have titled this section of the book "Pets Behaving Badly," or maybe "Wet Noses Can Lead You Astray." Either way, my point here is that your pet should be a goodwill ambassador while on the road. Because smaller pets such as rodents, birds, reptiles, amphibians, and, to some extent, cats travel in their cages or carriers, they naturally have a limited opportunity to offend, so the bulk of this chapter will demystify dog etiquette.

Woofing it down

If you're looking for a healthy treat or an impromptu meal for your traveling pet, head to the nearest convenience store or grocery and check out the baby-food aisle. Few pets can resist vitamin-packed, organic baby food. Cats and dogs can make a meal of beef, chicken, or fish; and all animals, from birds and reptiles to dogs and cats, will enjoy vitamin-packed green or orange puréed vegetables.

Petiquette® for Travel Hounds

When traveling, keep the comfort levels of others in mind. Even if your dog is exquisitely trained and under your voice control, others can still be intimidated by a strange dog running loose in a dog park or rest-stop area.

Walking the Dog

Moderately-paced walking and swimming are great exercises for your dog, and of

course, going on a walk will let her answer the call of nature. A brisk walk will build cardiovascular and muscle strength without putting undue stress on joints. A daily ten- to fifteen-minute walking or swimming session is a good start, and you can build to an hour a day if your pet seems up to it. If she can handle long, fast walks without fatigue after a few months, she could graduate to jogging with you.

Pay attention to areas marked off-limits to dogs, and keep the comfort of others in mind. Appropriate places to walk your dog when traveling include dog parks, roadside rest stops, and medians of streets and roads. Many of the large interstate rest stops include fenced dog parks, but if you need to make an emergency pit stop for your pooch, look for any exits advertising fast-food restaurants. You can usually find a grassy area bordering the parking lot of a franchise restaurant, or look for a roadside median or wide shoulder so that you can walk your dog as far

away from traffic as possible. And no matter where she goes, always carry a supply of plastic bags and pick up after her.

Keep a close eye on your dog when exercising her. Check for any unusual signs of fatigue or breathing trouble. If she wants to stop, let her. Just as those of us who are weekend warriors, dogs who overdo it can suffer strained tendons or ligaments, or other orthopedic problems.

For the sake of those around you and for your dog's safety, never allow your dog off-leash while traveling. Remember that even well-trained dogs can be startled into traffic in strange surroundings. When approaching other animals, ask their owner's permission before allowing your pet to "make friends," and do not assume that your pet will always be welcome when you go out with your friends—check with them first to make sure.

If you must go out when it's dark, put reflectors on your dog's collar and on your clothes. Walk or run on dirt paths or grass as much as possible. Gravel, concrete, asphalt, cinders, and road salt can irritate your pet's paws. If it's freezing cold, or hot and steamy out, either keep your outing short or play a little indoor fetch instead. The more active your dog is, the more water she will require, so make sure your pet has enough fresh water before and after your run. If you are going for a long jaunt, take some water along—for both of you.

no pet left behind pet etiquette

Cat Tracks

Unlike dogs, cats are designed for short, frequent periods of intense activity rather than longer, slower-paced exercise sessions. You'll find a wide selection of toys to help your cat become more active.

Anything light that moves easily across the floor can give your cat a chance to practice swatting and chasing. Balled-up paper works well in a pinch. Just make sure that your kitty isn't batting anything that she could chew up or swallow. The end of a moving string (a shoestring works great!) should bring out the predator in even the most sedentary cat. Empty boxes and paper bags are perfect "caves" for your cat to explore. But remember that plastic bags can cause suffocation—keep them out of your cat's reach.

Scratching is an activity that stretches and tones the muscles in your cat's shoulders and back, as well as cleans under her claws. It is not wise to allow your cat to roam a hotel room unattended if there is the slightest chance that she will scratch the furniture, but if she is accustomed to using a scratching post and you do not want to purchase one for the hotel room, a piece of corrugated cardboard can be a good replacement.

From the beginning of your relationship with your kitty, never use your hand or fingers as "bait." This teaches your pet that it is all right to scratch and bite hands.

Airport Petiquette®

It is always best to keep a low profile when accompanying your pet at the airport. Do not let him out of the carrier once you enter the airport terminal. If he is traveling with you in the passenger cabin, never take him out of his carrier during the flight.

Be sure to take your dog outside to eliminate before walking her in an airport. Some airports provide dog-walking areas, but to be safe, have plenty of wee-wee pads on hand. Even if you are a responsible pet parent and don't give your pet food for six hours before a flight or water within two hours of takeoff, sometimes your little friend still has to relieve himself. If your pooch is sending you signals that this is the case, you can use the wee-wee pads in the airplane rest room, allowing your dog to relieve himself quickly, calmly, and discreetly. Your dog will be very grateful.

If he must travel in the cargo hold, fasten a water bowl filled with frozen water to the door of her carrier. If you are carrying your pet through baggage check, politely and quietly inform the TSA agent at the security checkpoint that a pet is in the carrier so he is not exposed to x-rays. If you are asked to take your pet out of the carrier as you pass through security on your way to the gate, make sure that he is wearing a collar and leash or, better yet, a harness.

Woofing it down

A little crushed ice before takeoff will satisfy your pet's thirst without causing her to have to urinate. You can ask for a little ice from any of the airport's food shops.

Cabin vs. Cargo

I recommend bringing your pet with you in the passenger cabin when you fly. But if your pet exceeds the size or weight limit (see page 29), then this simply is not possible. Airlines usually accept a limited number of animals in the cabin—generally one pet per passenger and two to four animals total on the flight. A member of the airline's corporate staff can grant permission for two cats or two puppies from the same litter to travel in a single carry-on bag.

The Federal Aviation Administration (FAA) allows each airline to adopt a policy regarding the acceptance or non-acceptance of pets in the passenger cabin. The FAA does mandate that if a pet is accepted in the passenger cabin, the pet and carrier must fit securely under the seat in front of the passenger and that the complete floor area in the section is open and accessible in the event of an emergency. Additionally, passengers with pets are not permitted in the bulkhead or the Emergency Exit rows. See resources, page 164, for a list of airlines that accept pets in the cabin.

Most pets fly in the cargo hold as checked baggage when traveling with their owners or when they are being shipped unaccompanied. Some airlines do not ship pets as checked baggage at all, while others will accept them only as air cargo and only from a "known shipper"—licensed pet breeders, commercial shippers, or freight forwarders. The Animal Welfare Act (AWA) was enacted to ensure that animals traveling as cargo are treated humanely and not subjected to dangerous conditions.

Plane Sense

In the cargo hold, air space must be calculated for the number of live animals on the flight, so reserve space for your pet as checked baggage well before the flight. Live animals, whether in the cabin, as checked baggage, or as air cargo will be taken on a first-come, first-served basis. Once you have obtained a hard-sided container with ventilation on three sides that meets the requirements of the United States Department of Agriculture (USDA), be sure to make your pet reservation early and then confirm the reservation forty-eight hours before travel.

Inquire whether your pet can be hand-carried on and off the plane rather than being loaded on a conveyer belt, which is stressful for the pet and could also lead to accidental release or injury should the container fall off the belt (this is rare, but it does happen). Ask about "counter-to-counter" shipping, in which the animal is loaded immediately before departure and unloaded immediately after arrival.

Be certain that ground personnel are aware of your pet in the cargo hold so that actions can be taken if necessary (as in the case of a layover or long delay). Inform the captain and the flight crew that your pet is aboard. The flight crew must activate the temperature control for the cargo compartment as soon as the pet is loaded. If you experience long layovers or delays, do not be shy about asking the flight crew whether your pet has adequate shelter and ventilation. Tell the flight attendant that your pet is in

Troubleshooting

Crate-Door Security

An animal's crate door must remain unlocked during shipping, but you can ensure that your beloved pet will not be lost if the door is accidentally unlatched. Weave a tie-out cable with a clip at each end through the bars of the crate door and vents.

Animals that are very young, very old, pregnant, ill, or injured should not fly. Cats, snub-nosed dogs (pugs, Pekinese, boxers, and others), and long-nosed dogs (shelties, collies, greyhounds, and others) are prone to severe respiratory problems in an airplane's poorly ventilated cargo hold and should travel in the passenger cabin with his owner (if his size permits). Some airlines will not accept snub-nosed breeds if the temperature exceeds 70°F anywhere on the route.

the cargo hold. Ask to be told when your pet is safely on board so you can relax (don't forget to ask again if you change planes).

An airline cannot guarantee that it will accept a pet that it has not seen. Considerations for acceptance of pets include the pet's health and disposition. A health certificate from your vet will help to address any concerns. An airline must also determine that all paperwork is in order and that the crate meets all requirements. **Remember, the pet owner is responsible to ensure that all the proper paperwork is in order.**

Making sure the travel experience is stress-free for your pet is extremely important, so remember to leave extra time for checking in and paperwork, so that you are not rushing through the airport to make your flight.

Hotel Petiquette®

Even the most pet-friendly places have rules and regulations for animals. Be sure to follow them. For example, health regulations require that animals be kept out of areas where food is being prepared or served, but in many cases you can take a leashed pet into a sidewalk café. Swimming pools are usually off-limits. Although it seems almost obvious, your pet should be flea-free, both for your pet's sake and as a courtesy to future hotel guests.

Keep your pet quiet. If your pet is anxious and barks, meows, or screeches when left alone, it's best to take them with you when you leave your hotel room, to keep from invoking the ire of your neighbors and the staff. If the television has a calming effect, you can try leaving it on when your pet is left in the room to keep him company and muffle the sounds of people passing the door, and be sure to give him a long-lasting treat. Chewing releases calming endorphins, so a ham-scented nylon chew toy is ideal.

Do not let your pet damage hotel furniture. If you are not going to keep him in a container at night, bring sheets and bedspreads from home and cover hotel furniture and bedding. Clean up after your pet—inside and outside your room. Dispose of kitty litter and any other "accidents" properly—check with housekeeping. Do notify management if something is damaged, and be prepared to pay for repairs, and add a little extra to the housekeeping tip. And remember, only let your pet approach people if they express an interest in greeting and petting her.

Troubleshooting

If you plan a day trip that does not include your pet, make arrangements at the hotel for a dog walker while you are out, call a local pet store franchise to schedule a grooming session, or find out about the local doggie day camp.

the things p

ets do

We all look forward to sharing the thrills and discoveries of adventuring on the open road with our four-footed or feathered companions, but what if, despite your best training and preparation, your pet does not adjust well to travel or gets sick during a trip? Read on, because this chapter will help you prepare for and overcome all the potential scrapes, motion sickness, anxiety, and various other complaints of traveling pets.

Pet Behavior on the Road

Of course, the best way to address on-the-road behavior problems, such as anxiety or aggression toward other people or their pets, is to avoid them altogether by socializing your pet ahead of time. Cats and other small pets that are carrier-bound during travel are somewhat exempt from the need to socialize, but you can still acclimate them to car travel and even air travel over time (for tips on keeping small pets comfortable in their carriers during travel, see page 33). Because dogs are most likely to leave their carriers and accompany their owners during trips, we will focus on socializing advice for dogs, but if you are the owner of a particularly gregarious cat, parrot, rabbit, or ferret, you will find some tips here that you can adapt to those pets.

Some General Rules of Thumb

When traveling with your pet, the most basic road rule to remember is to use common sense. Anticipate and avoid problems by reminding yourself that it was you who invited your pet to come along and it is your responsibility to ensure that he is as safe and comfortable as possible.

Some of the first things to consider are food and water. All pets can be fussy and finicky when it comes to mealtime, so bring along your pet's preferred food, since it might not be available everywhere. It's also important to have adequate water for your pet. Sometimes water in new cities can upset his stomach or digestion. If you have any doubts about the water where you are going, then bring water from home or offer bottled or distilled water. You can also gradually mix the water from home with the new water.

Try to keep your regular feeding routine, but give your pet his main meal at the end of the day or when you've reached your destination in order to reduce the chances of motion sickness on the road. Plan to stop every two to four hours to let your dog or cat stretch her legs, have a drink, and answer nature's call (and always clean up after your pet!). Be sure your pet is leashed before opening the car door. It will keep him from

Teaching your dog the "down" command can help him stop barking. In a barking situation, put him in the "down" position. When a dog is lying down, it is actually physically difficult for him to bark.

breaking free and running away. Be sure he has a collar and ID tag, at a minimum, in case you become separated.

When you stop to eat on the road, it is best to go to a carryout place and eat in the car or at a picnic area near the restaurant. If you have a choice, opt for a drive-thru window restaurant. You should never leave your pet alone in a car, but if you must stop at a restaurant that doesn't permit pets, keep your car door window open and ask for a table near the window where you can keep an eye on your car and your pet.

Pet Stress Problems

Your pet depends on you to make her traveling experience a pleasant one. So before leaving, ask yourself what else you could bring along that will help make your pet comfortable and help keep her relaxed and happy. Have a Pet Emergency Preparedness Kit always on hand, and then all you have to add are perishable items such as food and medication, along with some of your pet's favorite toys, before you and she have an outing. For a list of emergency preparedness items to pack in your kit, see pages 80–81.

Noise Control

Even the best-behaved pets can sometimes become noisy in unfamiliar situations if they are not prepared for them. As they say, the best defense is a good offense—socializing your pet with people and other animals at a young age (or at the very least, well in advance of your trip), independent of the carrier, will help prevent him from barking, squawking, or hissing at wheelchairs, cars, kids, and other animals.

Whenever your pet is quiet, begin to condition him to stay quiet: Praise him, saying "Good boy, quiet!" He will learn to associate praise with being quiet. Keep in mind, too, that a tired dog is a quiet dog. Make sure yours has plenty of exercise before exposing him to a barking situation so that he is tired, relaxed, and happy. When he starts to bark, say

"Good boy, quiet," and hold a treat to his nose but don't give it to him for a second or two—it is impossible for a dog to lick a treat, or chew, and bark at the same time. Repeat the exercise as often as possible, certainly daily. Recruit friends or neighborhood kids to help by riding skateboards by as you walk him or by ringing your doorbell. It can take several weeks to turn around a persistent barker, but you can do it.

I cannot stress this point enough—never leave your pet alone in the car. Even on a pleasant day, inside-car temperatures can soar to well over 100°F in ten minutes if the car is parked in the sun, which can lead to heat stroke, brain damage, and death.

When the sun is strong, avoid strenuous activities with your dog, such as hiking, running, and fetch. Take care that your pet doesn't escape your watch and overheated, and keep lots of cool drinking water on hand. When traveling with your pet, keep a cool, wet towel in the car.

Symptoms of overheating include:

- Rapid, shallow breathing
- Heavy panting
- Skin hot to the touch
- Body temperature of 104°F or higher
- Excessive salivation
- Vomiting
- Unsteadiness/dizziness
- Glazed eyes
- Deep red or purple tongue and gums

Treatment:

- Place your pet in the shade.
- Dampen her head and neck with cool water.
- Give her small amounts of drinking water.
- Seek veterinary help if your pet's condition doesn't improve quickly.

no pet left behind the things pets do

Allowing your pet to get too cold—or to suffer hypothermia—is just as dangerous as overheating. As stated earlier, never leave your pet alone in a car. And take care that your pet doesn't escape your watch on a cold day. Always keep a dog sweater or jacket and a blanket in your car. If the ground is frozen, consider putting neoprene boots on your dog before walking her.

Symptoms of hypothermia include:

- Shivering
- Weakness
- Lethargy
- Skin cold to the touch
- Body temperature of 95°F or lower

Treatment:

- Move your pet to a warm environment.
- Quickly warm her by massaging her head, chest, and extremities.
- Bundle her in towels or warm blankets. Put a hot water bottle in the blankets to add heat.
- Immerse your pet in water that is 101 to 103°F
- Seek veterinary attention.

What not to do to a chilled pet:

- Do not allow your pet to chill if water was used to warm her.
- Do not burn your pet by using blankets, heating pads, water, etc., that are too hot and may damage her skin.
- Do not use excess superficial heat such as a fire or a space heater. This may cause superficial blood vessels to dilate, resulting in shock.

Motion Sickness and Other Automobile Concerns

I have been fortunate—neither Sherpa nor SuNae suffered from motion sickness. But many people do have to deal with this problem. Fortunately, motion sickness is something that most puppies outgrow. If you want to include your puppy or other pet in your active lifestyle, don't let your pet's tendency to become sick stop you from taking her in the car.

Part of an animal's tendency toward motion sickness stems from the stress or anxiety of riding in a car. Try to create positive experiences for your pet that she will associate with the car. Why not try a trip to a new park for a game of Frisbee or catch? A ride to a pet bakery? A trip to visit a favorite friend? Maybe your pet enjoys riding through the car wash with you. Sherpa used to love it when I sang in the car (even though I cannot hold a tune and my mother has told me never to let anyone hear me sing), and she would chime right in. SuNae enjoys my singing as well, but instead of joining me in a duet, she simply curls up and falls asleep.

Cats that don't travel very often can moan and wail all the way there and back. That's unpleasant for both of you; so I advise you, if you have a kitten, to start car training now, and he may soon take to it like, well, a fish to water. Be sure to keep your cat in a carrier while traveling, and invest in a squirm-proof halter and leash so that you can exercise him during long-distance trips.

Warning Signs and Treatments

Keep an eye on your pet. Usually the first signs of motion sickness are yawning or drooling. The good news is that a lot of the same things that help people overcome motion sickness also work for pets. If you stop the car and take your dog or cat out for a walk when you notice the warning signs, you can often prevent sickness, at least for a while. Cracking a window to increase ventilation in the back seat can help these pets and small, crate-bound pets too.

A teaspoon of puréed pumpkin mixed into your pet's food is a simple, safe treatment for diarrhea and can be administered two or three times a day, as needed, until your pet's condition improves. Shop for it in the pie section of the grocery, or for a travel-sized container, look in the baby food aisle.

Sometimes the churning juices in an empty stomach can make matters worse. If you see the warning signs, offer your pet an unsalted cracker or plain piece of bread. Other bland, calming foods you can offer any pet suffering from nausea or diarrhea include a little plain, boiled hamburger, rice, oatmeal, or the appropriate type of baby food for your pet species. Calm your pet by talking to him.

If diarrhea is present and if there are no other symptoms of illness, withhold food for two to four hours. Withhold both food and water if your pet is also vomiting, but do not withhold water for more than two hours. The time period for withholding food should be based on whether your pet is a normal, healthy adult versus a puppy or a kitten, an elderly pet, or a pet with any special or compromising conditions. (If your pet has diabetes or any other type of illness or medical condition, consult your veterinarian before withholding food and water.)

When you do resume feeding your dog or cat, the best home remedy for diarrhea is to serve a 50/50 mixture of boiled hamburger (drain off the water and fat) and plain cooked rice. A restaurant or hotel room service will be more than happy to help out here. Appropriate feedings are as follows:

$1/_4$ cup of mixture four times a day for cats and small dogs

$1/_2$ cup of mixture four times a day for medium dogs

$3/_4$ cup of mixture four times a day for large dogs

Your veterinarian may want to adjust the servings or may recommend a prescription diet instead.

Note the frequency and substance of the diarrhea. If symptoms persist for more than a day or two, or if they worsen or return, contact the pet's doctor immediately. Always check with your vet before giving your pet any over-the-counter medication. Your pet's species, medical history, and size will dictate the dosage and whether the medication is appropriate.

If you are not positive that motion sickness is the cause of your pet's illness, try to discover it. Causes can include changes in diet or water, infection, poisoning, or swallowing an obstructing object. If there is a chance that the cause could be more serious than motion sickness, consult a veterinarian immediately.

Other Causes, Other Cures

If your pet suffers simple motion sickness, and cannot seem to overcome it, you should also consult your veterinarian. Your vet will likely suggest that you withhold water for an hour before leaving for a trip (you can provide ice to keep him from becoming too thirsty), and then only feed your pet once you've completed the trip at the end of the day. If all else fails, he may suggest a small dosage of Dramamine® or a prescription tranquilizer that diminishes nausea; but make this a last-ditch remedy, and be sure to study the side effects of the medication because some side effects can be unpleasant or even life-threatening.

Perform Travel Health Checks

Perform a daily "health check" on your pet when away from home. In unfamiliar surroundings, your pet's appetite, energy, and disposition may change. Watch for unusual discharges from the nose and eyes, excessive scratching or biting of any body part, unusual lumps, limping, loss of appetite, abnormal elimination, or excessive water consumption. Visit a local veterinarian if you are concerned about any physical or behavioral changes.

part II

...go!

chapter 5

dom

estic
travel

If you are a "pathetic pet parent" like me, you don't want to wait for a big road trip—you want your pet by your side even on your days off, as you run your weekend errands. Whether you are traveling locally or across the country, you will find this chapter an invaluable guide to acclimating your pet to traveling, whether by car, bus, or plane, and whether for three, three hundred, or three thousand miles.

Traveling by Car

There is no better way to create wonderful memories than by taking a car trip with the ones you love. And with a little practice, your pet will look forward to spending quality time with his best friend on road trips large and small. He will listen raptly as you ramble on about the sights and experiences you enjoy together and will share your interest in the passing scenery. Your pet can be part of your delight in hiking and camping, or a companion as you run errands.

Prepare with Basics

Put your pet in your place—you wouldn't attempt to take up a new sport like scuba diving, skiing, or kayaking without taking a short, hands-on course. Now that you have acclimated your pet to his carrier, it's time to take a few practice spins around the block to get the hang of car travel. Most of the time, your "car time" is spent running local errands. So do start your pet with car rides ranging from a half-hour to an hour, and don't wait until you have to take him to the vet—make training fun for both of you. Go on short errands together, and take your pet where she is sure to be rewarded.

Begin with trips that allow you to stay with your pet, because getting used to being in a car for the first time is stressful enough for her, without putting her in a situation where she feels abandoned in a strange place. Great first destinations include drive-in banks and fast-food restaurants, which often include a dog cookie or cat treat with the transaction when a four-footed passenger is on board. Drive your furry or feathered companion to pet-friendly stores, such as pet shops or garden centers, where she will get lots of attention and be stimulated by interesting sights, sounds, and smells. Chauffeur her to a park for a special outing or to a sidewalk café where you can enjoy a treat together. Pets are quick learners; after only a few special outings, they become excited to see you take out the car keys.

A note of warning: while it may look cute in the movies, do not allow your pet to ride with his head out of the window or, worse, in the open bed of a truck, because stones, glass, and dust can blow into his eyes and sudden stops can cause injuries. A loose pet in the car is distracting and dangerous for the driver, as well. One time when I was traveling in Maine with Sherpa, she was jumping nimbly from the front of the car to the back of the car and then decided it might be fun to climb under my feet and try her paw at the pedals. I immediately recognized the danger in this situation and pulled over to the side of the road to put Sherpa into her carrier. For safety's sake, always properly restrain your pet in a carrier or car-approved security harness (for more information, see page 24).

(for more information, see page 24).

Woofing it down

Carrots are good for your dog; they sweeten breath, settle queasy stomachs, and provide vitamins. Best of all, dogs like them; so after a leg-stretch stop, reward yourself and your intrepid traveler with carrot sticks, crisp from the cooler.

Short Car Trips

When your pet becomes a comfortable passenger, it is time to teach him to wait calmly in the car while you go into a store. This is also a good time to teach the "stay" command. She should know that she must sit still while you snap her leash on (while the doors are still closed) and wait for you to give the "come" command (after you open a door) before she can exit the car. Teach her to stay in only one seat. This way she won't run to another seat and jump out a door being opened by another passenger.

Begin by going where you can keep an eye on him. Try a coffee or snack shop where you can park near a window or a pet shop where they will understand that you are training your pet. Crack the car windows for ventilation, quietly tell your pet to wait, and hand over a special chewy treat or chew toy—chewing constructively occupies cats and parrots, and studies have shown that chewing releases calming endorphins in dogs (better for him to calm himself with a nylon bone than your car seats).

Do not make a fuss when you leave; quietly inside, stand by the window or order a latte and sit where you can observe. If you see that your pet seems agitated or is barking, go out and reassure him that you are nearby, and then return to the store for a few more minutes. Repeat this as often as needed, extending your stay each time until the animal can calmly wait for up to twenty minutes. Animals have short attention spans, and I recommend that you always check on your pet frequently and never leave any pet alone in a car for longer than a few minutes—and only when the car is parked in the shade and outdoor temperatures are moderate. Within this time frame, you can complete myriad errands ranging from dropping off dry cleaning and charity donations to returning a DVD and picking up the kids at soccer practice. Your pet will learn to look forward to sharing these little adventures with you and eventually will enjoy traveling for the sake of travel.

Basic Car Supplies

If you take your dog on frequent short car trips, be sure to keep some pet essentials in the car. In addition to your Pet-Preparedness Kit (see page 80), you also need supplies to make your pet's ride safe and comfortable. A cover designed to create a hammock between the front and back seats will prevent your pet from being thrown to the floor during sudden stops. I recommend a halter; it is more secure than a collar, which can slip off an excited or frightened pet. There are harnesses designed for pets as small as reptiles, birds, and cats. Keep an extra leash in the glove compartment, just in case. If you dedicate a pet bed to the car, you can keep it where you want your pet to stay and be reasonably certain that she will get the idea.

Carriers are, of course, an absolute necessity. When it comes to carriers for small dogs and cats, my choice is the soft-sided carrier. I wouldn't use anything else. My dog Sherpa loved her carrier, as do my current dogs SuNae and Kartu. They have a strap specifically designed to run a seat belt through, roll-up and roll-down flaps for privacy, and a travel tray that slides in and out. Some soft-sided models also include

wheels for even more ease of travel. Other innovative products for creatively restraining your smaller pet in the car include companion seats and portable mesh containers. You can find any of these products online and in many pet stores.

The only car-carrier option for large dogs is a hard-sided crate. You'll find hard-sided containers to suit every need, including stationary models, folding ones, some with double doors or triple doors, others with divider panels, and designer containers that have cushioning. Hard-sided containers can be used in the cargo area of a station wagon, SUV, or minivan, or in the back seat of a car (depending on the size of the dog and the container). Hard-sided containers are a safe, portable option for traveling with your pet, but some can be quite cumbersome (for properly sizing a container, see page 28).

An alternative for a large dog that's both safe and comfortable is a car halter and seat belt combination. It enables your pet to either sit or lie down safely, and protects both your pet and the car's passengers. A car harness is most suited to short trips—it may restrict movement more than a properly sized carrier (for sizing, see page 28). The potential disadvantages to this type of harness system are that it may not work outside the car or on airplanes, and if your pet experiences motion sickness, you'll need to protect your upholstery.

The barrier is another option for restraining pets in a car. Barriers are built into some new model cars, while others are adjustable and will fit most car models. A lot of people find the barrier effective because once it's installed in your car, it's a fast and easy way to transport your pets—particularly if you have several large dogs and there's not enough room for multiple carriers. The only downside to a barrier is that while it keeps the pet contained and away from the driver, it offers no added safety for your pets if the car is involved in an accident. Upon impact, pets could suffer serious, or even fatal, injuries if they are hurled against the barrier or the side of the car.

Make a Pet-Preparedness Kit

Your pet depends on you to make his traveling experience a pleasant one. Before leaving home, ask yourself what else you could bring along that would help make your pet comfortable and keep him relaxed and happy. Have a Pet-Preparedness Kit always on hand, and then all you have to add are perishable items, such as medication and some of your pet's favorite toys, before you and your pet have an outing.

Purchase a backpack, small duffel bag, or any other zippered tote, fill it with the supplies listed below, and keep it inside the carrier, which you should store with your suitcases or in your car, if your pet is a frequent traveler.

- A waterproof container, such as a sealable plastic food storage box, with:
    - Copies of pedigree, license, medical, and vaccination records
    - Contact information for your pet's vet, kennel, and breeder
    - Your cell phone number and another emergency contact's phone number
    - Photos of your pet labeled with his or her name
    - Feeding instructions
    - Styptic powder
    - A travel-sized pet health-care book
    - Flashlight
- Halter and leash (for dog, cat, bird, ferret, or lizard)
- Cleanup supplies:
    - Disposable garbage bags and paper towels
    - Liquid dish soap and disinfectant
- Blanket to protect your pet from cold temperatures and for scooping up a fearful pet to place into the pet carrier; a pillowcase or EvackSack (a rubberized mesh bag for transporting cats and puppies) will work, as well
- Muzzle (for an injured animal)
- Long leash and yard stake

- Litter bags and an absorbent, washable liner, such as the Sherpa Liner® (for dog or cat), along with bagged litter and disposable litter box (for cat), wee-wee pads (for dog), or newspapers (cage liners for birds and reptiles)
- Unbreakable food and water bowls
- Sealed dry or canned food (for dog or cat), seed mixes and supplements (for birds and reptiles) (Note: Refresh these supplies quarterly.)
- Bottled water (Note: Refresh these supplies quarterly.)
- One or two durable toys, including a chew toy for dogs and birds in the parrot family
- Jacket or raincoat (for dog or cat)
- Brush, flea shampoo, or other grooming aids

Traveling Babies Need TLC

- Don't plan car travel with a pet in extremely hot or cold weather.
- Do park in the shade, and leave the air conditioning or heater running if you must transport the pet in extreme temperatures.
- Don't attach a pet's collar to a seat belt, clothes rack, or door handle—sudden stops could cause a neck injury.
- Don't put a pet in the front seat where she is vulnerable to air-bag injuries.
- Do use a between-seat barrier or cushioned car harness that can be fastened to the back seat belt for short trips.
- Do put a pet carrier in the back seat for longer trips. If possible, position the carrier door so that the pet can see you through the opening between the front seats.
- Don't put a carrier in the cargo area of your car where it will be vulnerable to being rear-ended.
- Do keep bottled water in the car, and offer your pet a drink at each stop.

Making Car Travel Safe for Birds and Cold-Blooded Pets

The car may seem like a friendly place for a bird, reptile, or amphibian, but it can harbor hazards. These small creatures react adversely to pollutants, so extend your pet-safe home maintenance habits to the car. Your best option is to clean the interior with nontoxic, pet-approved soap and water, and then vacuum (not shampoo) the carpets. Avoid aerosols, fumy cleaners, and air fresheners. Feathered, finned, and scaly pets require species-specific temperatures, so adjust the heat or air conditioning accordingly, and place the cage away from windows and vents to avoid drafts.

Purchase a safe, travel-approved carrier or cage, and be sure to put house chewers in a cage with stainless steel or non-toxic enameled bars. If your pet appears agitated by traffic, cover the cage with a breathable cloth cover to make her feel secure. Set the cage in the back seat, not on the floor, to reduce vibrations, and strap it securely to a seat belt. For additional stability, you can encircle the cage and seat back with an elastic bungee cord. For short trips (a half-hour or less), offer a spill-proof, juicy treat such as salad greens or fruit rather than water or food. For longer trips, attach a tube or siphon-style water bottle to the grill of the crate, and provide palatable, high-energy foods, such as spray millet or "vacation" food for cold-blooded animals, which will stay fresh for several hours.

If you want to travel with a cockatiel, parrot, or chicken (which are gaining popularity as suburban pets), look into purchasing a bird halter and leash, which you can attach to a backpack or belt loop when you and your buddy leave the car. These gregarious birds will happily sit on your shoulder and take in the sights as you hike, but if startled, they can take flight. If that happens, a bird harness and leash can save you a lot of heartache. I recommend transporting smaller songbirds and finches, which are skittish by nature, in covered cages and only as necessary, such as to the vet or during a move. You can also buy bird diapers to protect your clothes and the car.

City Travel—Hopping a Taxi, Subway, or Bus

Urban pets, when accompanied by their owners, can adroitly hop a taxi to doggy day care, groomer, or vet. Hailing a taxi for you and your best friend or even taking a bus or subway can be a challenge in the city, however. In most cases, getting around town on public transport depends on the kindness of train conductors and bus drivers.

Some taxi drivers do not want pets in their car, so it is best to call the carrier and ask in advance. Remember that taxi and limo drivers aren't obliged to transport your pet— but many will. The smaller your pet, the better your chances. The key is to be polite. Ask the driver if he would not mind, and reassure him that your pet is clean, well mannered, and quiet. Most important, remember to tip well. For a small fee, most limousine companies allow you to bring along your pet, as long as you give notice when making a reservation.

no pet left behind domestic travel

Dogs or cats in carriers and bags (particularly if they're stylish) are frequently allowed on the city's subways and buses. That said, there is a restriction that states "no big dogs." Unfortunately, there is no official definition of what constitutes a "big dog," which is to say that the conductor's discretion decides whether a big dog gets on or not. So be smart: travel with your hound during off-peak hours. A friend of mine gets away with taking her dog on the subway in a shopping cart. With a little effort, you can take your urban hound just about anywhere.

If all else fails, call a pet taxi. Urban pet taxis offer the best of everything; some are combined with boarding and grooming services, or pet ambulances complete with stretchers, blankets, and water. The cost in major cities is about a dollar a block. One company in San Francisco charges $40 per hour. Some even go the distance, such as driving a dog from New York City to Florida for about $4,000. You must book these special taxis in advance. Another option: some pet sitters include a taxi fee to take pets to the groomer or vet. Some have a flat charge plus mileage if the trip is more than ten miles (see resources, page 176).

Long Trips

In "dog years," any trip that takes several hours or longer qualifies as a long trip. In most cases, your long car trip is all about enjoying the family vacation with all the members of your family—including your pet. But sometimes, the

Troubleshooting

Clipping a Bird's Wings

Parrots, chickens, and other heavy birds usually fold their wings and prefer to walk rather than fly, but when startled, they can suddenly dart skyward. Whether you travel with finches, canaries, or big birds, it is a good idea to clip one or both wings to keep them from becoming lost. Clipping feathers, like cutting hair, is painless, and the feathers will grow back during the next molt. The new style of clipping uses pet-toenail clippers to trim just a few flight feathers from the center section of the wing, which is less traumatic and unsightly than older methods. When the bird folds his wings against his body, the trimmed feathers are invisible.

Although it's often overlooked, grooming is an important part of your pet's health program. Routine brushing and combing prevents matting and removes loose hair and dirt from furry pets. If you have a bird or reptile, it cleans his skin and washes off parasites. Don't forget to offer these pets a bowl of water to bathe in. Because it stimulates the blood supply to the skin, grooming also gives your pet a healthier and shinier coat, skin, or feathers. Dog grooming should not be overlooked when you are on vacation. If you normally take your dog to a groomer and wish to do so while you're on vacation, you can find a directory of U.S. and international groomers at www.findagroomer.com.

car trip is the result of your limited choices; your pet may be too exotic to be accepted by airlines or other carriers, your dog may be too large to move through an airport in a carrier, or you may just not want a large or exotic pet enduring the discomforts of a plane's cargo compartment.

Assessing How Your Pet Handles Travel

I do not recommend taking your pet on a two-week holiday if he has never gone farther than the neighborhood park or ventured past your front door. Getting him used to the car by taking short trips first is a must.

Before you make plans for your long holiday, it is important to consider your pet's temperament and personality. Does he make friends easily? Is he trusting with strangers and affectionate toward children? Does he hiss, growl, or snap at your neighbor's cat, or bark, yowl, or screech at strangers and strange noises? These are all factors that you must consider when planning your first vacation together.

Gearing up for the Road

If you need to plan and pack ahead for your car trip, you also need to do so for your pet. In addition to a carrier, harness, or barrier, you'll also need to bring the Pet-Preparedness Kit (see page 80), making sure that you have replenished the water and food in it, if you haven't used the Kit for a while. Make sure your pet's vaccinations are up-to-date and that you have reviewed the regulations on crossing state lines along your route. Finally, remember to adjust the car's air conditioning or heat with pet comfort in mind.

Leg-Stretching Strategies

It bears repeating that pets have short attention spans, and even the most patient will eventually become road weary. Your pet should be allowed out and about whenever possible. Letting him stretch his legs and have some fun time out of the carrier will make him more accepting of the time he has to spend in it. The best coping strategy is to schedule exercise breaks every couple of hours, plus whenever nature calls. For the sake of safety, avoid stopping along the road; look for official road-side rest stops. Most have designated tree-shaded, grassy pet-walking areas, which are well away from picnic areas, and all will require that you keep your pet leashed and clean up after her. Indoor food-court rest stops along major highways are the ultimate; generally these offer the added safety of a fenced-in dog park. Cats actually dislike strange places, and may be happier left in their travel crate than stretching their legs at a busy rest stop. If this is the case, buy a carrier that is large enough to hold a disposable litter box. If experience tells you that your cat cannot relax for the ride, you may need to seek a tranquilizer from your vet (see page 107).

Did You Know?

Although you should not feed your dog or cat after bedtime the night before you hit the road (in order to avoid car sickness), birds are an exception. Birds have high metabolisms, so you should always have food available for them.

Pet-Friendly Motels

These days it is not difficult to find pet-friendly chain motels across the country, but you should anticipate your arrival and call ahead at least twenty-four hours to reserve a room, because these rooms are usually in short supply. If you have a favorite motel chain, check its Web site or call its toll-free number to locate franchises along your route. A great source of pet-friendly hotels and accommodations in the city or town of your choice is www.petfriendly.com. If you are an AAA member, also check the AAA list of pet-friendly hotel/motel chains.

Camping with Pets

Camping is an ideal vacation to share with pets because most enjoy exploring the scents and sounds of the wilderness, and camping is less strenuous than hiking for an older or less-fit pet. Give yours an orientation course before going by setting up your tent in the back yard for a week before your trip. When she is used to this new "intruder" in the yard, put her bed inside the tent, sit beside it, and invite her in. It may be helpful to bribe her with a treat or two, and be sure to praise her for coming in. It also helps to take your pet to local parks, fish hatcheries, or nature preserves for short hikes to get her in the right mindset. It goes without saying that your pet should mind her manners when camping: no barking, charging other dogs, jumping on people, or other rude dog behavior. See the section on obedience (pages 40–41) if your pet needs to brush up her etiquette.

Dog accoutrements should be more durable than fancy. While camping, store pet food in a critter-proof container with a locking lid. Look for, and use, the biodegradable "pet pick-up" bags in rustic wooden dispensers, which are situated around camps, rest stops, and nature preserves. Keep your pet leashed. Even if he is well-behaved, he can rouse the ire of a wild animal, such as a bear, bobcat, predator bird like a great horned owl or hawk, or the sharp antlers of deer, elk, or moose. To allow your pet some free movement, create a zip line-type tether by stringing a commercial dog cable between trees at your campsite. I recommend that you fasten his leash to the line and to a halter, which is more secure than a collar. Never leave him unattended while he is outside, and do not let him sleep outside alone at night.

In cold weather, outfit your short-haired dog in a jacket or sweater, especially at night, and place a sheet of plastic under his bed to keep it dry and warm. If you plan to hike over rough or icy terrain, pick up a pair of neoprene dog booties. And remember to take your Pet-Preparedness Kit (see page 80) when you camp. For a list of the top pet-friendly national parks, see resources, page 177.

Roadside Rescues

No matter how prepared you are for your trip, the unexpected can still happen. Motion sickness, aches, pains, cuts, and scrapes can all crop up. Luckily, you don't have to carry an entire veterinary office with you when you travel. There are over-the-counter remedies that can treat your pet as well as you.

NOTE: Consult your vet before traveling to make sure any home remedies are safe and to verify dosages.

Helpful "people food"

- *Soda crackers* for settling stomachs of dogs, cats, and parrots
- *Plain oatmeal* for settling stomachs of dogs
- *Plain yogurt* for balancing the digestive systems of dogs and cats

Helpful Over-the-Counter Remedies

- *Buffered Aspirin* (never synthetic pain killers) for dogs only can be used for pain relief and as an anti-inflammatory. Aspirin is not tolerated well in puppies and should never be used for cats
- *Benadryl®* for itch relief for dogs. It can also be used for bee stings, insect bites, and injection-site reactions. Antihistamine creams or sprays can also be used (be sure to apply only where it cannot be licked off)
- *Dramamine®* for preventing car-sickness
- *Pepto-Bismol®* for settling stomachs, reducing gas, and stopping diarrhea— but should be used only for dogs
- *Mineral Oil* for easing constipation in dogs and cats and preventing hairballs in cats
- *Hydrogen Peroxide* (3 percent) for inducing vomiting if your dog ingests poison
- *Antibiotic Cream* (such as Neosporin®) for cuts and scrapes

To prevent infection and help cuts and scrapes heal, clean the area with a mild soap (try no-tears baby shampoo) and water, rinse, dry, and then apply an antibiotic cream. The same treatment works for smaller animals, birds, and reptiles that may cut their feet in their cages.

While all of these medications work for dogs, cats, birds, and even reptiles, fish are a different story—they need their own specific medication. If your fish is missing scales, or has a patch of fuzzy fungus, purchase medication from a pet shop that can be added to the aquarium water, and make sure that the water is at the ideal temperature. If you have one injured fish in a tank with healthy ones, remove it and isolate it in a smaller "hospital tank" until it recovers.

Interstate Travel Regulations

Anyone who plans to travel to another state with her pet needs to have Certificate of Veterinary Inspection (CVI). This official document is a health certificate signed by a licensed and accredited veterinarian. It guarantees that the pet shows no signs of communicable disease and gives a date that the inspection (examination) took place. This document should include rabies vaccination information with the date that the rabies shot was given.

Rabies vaccination documentation is required by all states for dogs and by most states for cats. States that currently do not require rabies vaccination documentation for cats are Arizona, California, Illinois, Iowa, Michigan, and Oklahoma. A CVI for dogs is required by all states except California and Texas. Cats are currently exempt from this requirement in California, Illinois, Montana, Texas, and Vermont. Of course, these are general recommendations. I recommend that you contact the particular state's agricultural or veterinary department directly for updated information before you travel.

You may be surprised to learn that, even in the United States, there are monkey-free states and no-ferret zones. Whether you are considering interstate or foreign travel with your hedgehog, chinchilla, sugar glider, ferret, or other "exotic" pet, your first step should be to check with your airline or travel company to ensure that your pet is acceptable for travel. Further information can be obtained from the USDA's Animal and Plant Health Inspection Service (APHIS). For contact information, see resources, page 197.

For more information about state requirements see resources, page 197.

In addition to your CVI certificate, for travel within the United States, your pet needs to have a health certificate from your veterinarian dated within ten days of departure stating that your pet is fit to travel. The health certificate and your pet's vaccination certificates should be attached to the kennel. Always carry extra copies on your person, in case you are asked to produce them. It's a good idea to keep an extra in your carry-on bag, in case one is misplaced.

If your pet is tranquilized before travel, your veterinarian must supply the name of the drug, the dosage, and how the drug was administered. This information should be included with the pet's health certificate and other veterinary paperwork, and a copy of this information should also be attached to the kennel.

Flying Domestically

Air travel is generally the quickest route between two points, and you have a wide choice of airlines that accept pets. While small dogs and cats are generally allowed in the cabin, large dogs are often required to be checked as baggage. Baggage holds can become hazardous if pets are exposed to extreme heat or cold for extended periods because they miss flights or planes are delayed. There is no way for owners to assist baggage-checked pets during flight. For this reason, the United States government recently required better training in pet handling for airline employees, and airlines must now notify the Department of Transportation about incidents involving animals.

What can you do to make things better? Check with the airline in advance to see whether your pet can be carried on the plane and travel in the passenger compartment. With your pet safely tucked under the seat in front of you, you can monitor his condition all during the flight. If not, flying off hours will lessen the stress of taking your pet into a crowded, noisy airport.

For the most comfortable air travel for any pet during the summer, choose early morning or evening flights to avoid high temperatures. During the winter, avoid near frigid temperatures by taking daytime flights. Always try to book non-stop flights to avoid potentially traumatic transfers or delays on the tarmac, and avoid flying during heavy traffic times, such as weekends and holidays.

When you arrive at your destination, promptly pick up your pet at baggage check and take him outside for fresh air and a walk.

Airline and Import Rules for Cold-Blooded Pets

Like small dogs, reptiles, amphibians, and turtles fit into most carry-on bags, but unfortunately most airlines do not recognize them as domesticated pets and will not allow them in the passenger cabin. Some passengers are not comfortable knowing that your pet iguana is traveling in the same row. Large snakes and reptiles weighing more than fifteen pounds must travel as cargo, but many airlines prohibit poisonous reptiles even in air cargo. Always check with your airline before arriving at the airport to see whether your pet can travel, and how. Also check with the USDA-APHIS Veterinary Services (www.aphis.usda.gov) for specific airline, state, and foreign country travel requirements.

Other suggestions for traveling with reptiles:

• Consider a lock on the travel container if your pet is traveling in the cabin with you. These pets can be great escape artists, but federal regulations do not allow locks on containers in the cargo hold of the aircraft. Instead, weave a leash through the door and air vents, and fasten the snap to the looped end of the leash.

• Never leave your pet unattended.

• Mark the traveling container "Do Not Touch" to avoid any unexpected surprises.

• Consider sending your pet via FedEx, UPS, or USPS rather than taking him in the cabin or putting him in cargo. (It may be less stressful for both of you.)

Airline Rules for Birds

Citing concern about avian influenza, some airlines and transportation companies no longer allow birds to travel in the cabin. Always check with your airline or travel company to ensure that your bird is accepted. Contact USDA-APHIS Veterinary Services to be certain you have all necessary documentation for your trip. The resources pages in the back of this book also provide quick references for the types of birds accepted on popular United States and foreign airlines.

Checklist

If you need to transport a puppy, kitten, or other baby mammal, be aware that the United States Department of Agriculture (USDA) requires that animals be at least eight weeks old and fully weaned for five days before travel.

internati

chapter 6

onal
travel

Having homes on both sides of the pond, my pets are quite accustomed to traveling abroad. Still, many pet owners are apprehensive about taking their furry friend with them on trips to another country—the fear of different foods, long flights, regulations, and the dreaded word "quarantine" keep most people from even considering taking their pet with them. While it is true that there are many rules and regulations that must be followed, and unfortunately, no magic carpet will deliver you and your pet to your dream locale without the required forms and documentation, traveling with your pet to exotic places can be a wonderful experience. This chapter will teach you what guidelines you must follow for international travel and how you can overcome all of those fears so that you can bring your best friend on the trip of your lives!

no pet left behind international travel

Happily, traveling with your pet into Canada or Mexico, or from Canada or Mexico into the United States—is a fairly uncomplicated experience if you have your papers and your pet's papers in order.

Also happily, traveling with your pet to popular destinations such as France, Great Britain, and Italy is becoming much more accepted and widespread. However, there are some destinations such as Hawaii, Tokyo, Osaka, Hong Kong, Beijing, Manila, and Guam that still have stringent restrictions on the types of pets accepted and how they can be transported into the country. Some destinations may require quarantines of up to six months. Violations of these restrictions can result in the confiscation or even the destruction of your pet. For the most up-to-date information, contact the Embassy or Consulate general office for each country on your itinerary—and be sure to begin this process at least four weeks before departure (see resources, page 190).

Microchips and Foreign Travel

While I recommend inserting microchips in all pets, it is absolutely essential to have a microchip inserted in all animals traveling internationally, especially to Europe—some countries require it. If you are planning a trip to Europe, your pet's microchip must be the ten-digit Avid® Euro Chip or the HomeAgain® chip. The one exception at this time is France, which requires a fifteen-digit chip. Immigration has universal scanners, but since the ISO ten-digit chip is the standard for Europe, most shelters use an ISO scanner. For more information on microchips, see page 201.

The European Experience

Europe is a paradise for pets; you see pets nearly everywhere you look. I especially enjoy seeing so many dogs walking off-leash, contentedly heeling next to their owners—in parks, stores, hotels, cafés, and barber shops. With the exception of Spain, dogs and cats are permitted on trains. Sometimes they must be in a carrier (usually cats). Often, dogs simply must be wearing a muzzle or just have to be leashed. Pets normally travel on trains for half-fare. The Eurail pass also includes certain ferries, buses, and steamers in the cost of the pass. Make sure you confirm current policies for all modes of transportation in advance.

Great Britain does not participate in the Eurail system, and the BritRail pass doesn't allow pets. Eurostar, the high-speed system connecting London, Paris, and Brussels, does not permit pets. If traveling by train in Europe, contact the appropriate agency for current policies (see resources, page 199).

Availability of Pet Food Abroad

When traveling overseas with your pet, avoid stomach upsets by keeping to your regular feeding routine and bringing along as much of your pet's preferred food as possible—it might not be available at your destination. It's also important to have adequate water from home or to offer distilled water.

Before you do run out of food and water from home, buy a good local brand of pet food and gradually mix the familiar with the new to help your pet adjust. In major European cities, you can find some familiar United States brands of foods. To find American pet products anywhere in the world, visit www.expatboxes.com. But should you find yourself without access to acceptable pet food, offer your pet basic human foods, such as a plain steak (cut into bite-sized pieces), hamburger (or hamburger mixed with rice), poached or hardboiled chopped eggs, or bite-sized pieces of chicken or organ meats such as giblets and liver.

The Differences between American and European Pet Food

When traveling in Europe, your pet could be eating better than she does at home. Why? Because pet food imported into Europe from the United States is required under the Animal Plant Health Inspection Services (APHIS) European certification system to be made from all human-grade ingredients. You may want to look for this

certification while still in the States because pet food manufacturers that have APHIS European certification labeled products use this as a means to assure customers of the high quality of their product's ingredients.

European Health Facilities

Europeans have had a long head start over the United States when it comes to having house pets and caring for them. Consequently, European pets have developed a high standard of living, being accepted in most businesses, including many restaurants, and public transportation. So it's not surprising that in the United Kingdom and on the European Continent, excellent veterinary services are available—although they can be expensive compared to United States vet costs.

If your pet takes medication, whether for something as serious as diabetes or as simple as allergies, by all means ask your vet to supply enough medication to last through your vacation. If you should run out or lose the medication, or if your pet becomes sick or injured abroad, you should have no trouble locating a veterinarian abroad who can prescribe what your pet needs.

In the British Isles, the Royal Society for the Prevention of Cruelty to Animals (RSPCA), the equivalent of the ASPCA in America, offers many pro-pet programs, including animal-care and pet-insurance information and aid for those who cannot afford the cost of animal medical care. For more information, visit www.rspca.org.uk/. The People's Dispensary for Sick Animals (PDSA) is a British charity veterinary care program to aid those who cannot afford the health care costs for their pets; find out more at www.pdsa.org.uk/.

Differences in American and Foreign Pet Customs and Protocol

In Europe and other European-language countries, pets are generally well behaved and respond to obedience commands, so it bears repeating that if yours is less than mannerly, take her to obedience school before heading out. In some lesser developed countries, pets are few and not well thought of. If you plan to visit one of these places with your pet, check on rules and regulations, keep her close by, and maintain a low profile.

But in Europe, your pet can benefit from the pet perks. For example, dogs dining at French restaurants with their owners quite often sit in a chair at the table with their own plate of food! Pets travel on trains, and if the pets are small enough, their owners carry them in bags to avoid paying for a pet ticket. A drawback of all this love? You must "mind the footpaths" in France; careless owners allow dogs to soil the paths, causing six hundred slips and falls per day!

Flying with Your Pet Internationally

Before taking a pet to another country, always contact that country's consulate or embassy for information concerning their requirements. Every country has specific health requirements for the entry of animals and most countries, including those of the European Union, have a veterinary certificate specific to their country. If foreign countries do not have written policies specifically addressing your species of pet, I strongly advise that you obtain something in writing from both the country's embassy and your chosen airline carrier to avoid potential problems.

If the country you are visiting does not have its own health certificate, you should use the International Health Certificate USDA-APHIS 7001 form, known as the United States Interstate and International Certificate of Health Examination for Small Animals. Some countries require that it be certified by the USDA.

The certification should include a description of the pet, state that she is healthy and free of parasites, and list the inoculations she has received, including the type, the manufacturer, and the batch number, if possible. The rabies shot must be given at least thirty days before travel and not more than twelve months before travel. Some countries require that the certificate be translated into the language of that country. Your area veterinarian-in-charge can provide you with the current regulations, tests, and inspections required.

When traveling with your pet to any of the countries of the European Union, you must use the new EU Form 998 Veterinary Certificate. Your vet will complete and sign the form, confirming vaccination information and that the pet is parasite-free and in good health. You must then take or mail the original form to the APHIS area office—called a Veterinary Service (VS) Area Office—in your state so that they can endorse and stamp it. This office can also assist you with questions relating to traveling with your pet, help you locate an accredited veterinarian, and inform you of the fees for the USDA endorsements and current export requirements.

For Web sites and information regarding USDA certificate forms, individual regulations, Veterinary Service Area Offices, and embassy information, see the resources section, pages 197–199.

Feeding and Watering Schedule for Air Travel

If forecasted temperatures are below 45°F, a Certificate of Acclimation must be issued by your vet stating that your pet can travel in that temperature. (Always check with the airline before booking passage to see whether it will accept this certificate.) If your pet does not require food or water on the flight, a signed statement from your veterinarian must be provided.

Food and water must be provided to puppies and kittens (eight to sixteen weeks old) every twelve hours. Mature pets must be fed every twenty-four hours and given water every twelve hours.

no pet left behind international travel

It is not a good idea to ship your pet in the cargo hold on a full stomach because she could be uncomfortable or, worse, become nauseous and soil her carrier. The USDA does, however, require you to offer your pet food and water within four hours before check-in with the airline—just don't overfeed her. When you check in with the airline, you must sign a certification of the time when you last offered food and water to your pet.

Food and water dishes designed to be used with crates (and which are available at most pet shops) must be securely attached to the carrier container door and be accessible to caretakers without their having to open the container. (Do not leave food or water in the dish; it will spill and make travel unpleasant for your pet.) Instructions for feeding and watering the animal over a twenty-four-hour period must be attached to the carrier. With the airline's approval, attach some of your pet's own dry food to be used for feeding. A healthy dog or cat can, if necessary, go twelve to eighteen hours without food or water.

The Tranquilizer Controversy

If your pet just cannot seem to overcome motion sickness, you should consult your veterinarian. Your vet will probably first suggest that you withhold water for an hour before leaving for a trip and that you feed your pet once you've completed the trip at the end of the day. The vet may also recommend medication for dogs or cats (but not for smaller animals, birds, or cold-blooded pets). While medications can definitely reduce motion sickness or anxiety, they also involve some risks and side effects.

Unfortunately, overtranquilizing a pet is common and the outcome is sometimes fatal. If your pet is tranquilized and must travel in the cargo compartment of a plane (which I do not recommend), your veterinarian must supply the name of the drug, the dosage, and how the drug was administered. This information should be included with the pet's health certificate and other veterinary paperwork.

National and international air transportation organizations, as well as the American Humane Association and the American Veterinary Medical Association, discourage tranquilizing pets before travel. An animal's ability to maintain balance is compromised by sedation, causing potential injury when the crate is moved by airline personnel. High altitudes for pets traveling in both cabin and cargo can create respiratory and cardiovascular problems for tranquilized pets, especially for snub-nosed dogs and cats.

The Pet Travel Scheme (PETS)

Island nations, such as Australia and the United Kingdom, which are rabies-free, have adopted the Pet Travel Scheme (PETS) to allow entry for dogs and cats from the United States and Canada without the usual six-month quarantine. To qualify, an APHIS-Accredited Veterinarian must issue the PETS Entry or Re-entry Certificate for pet cats and dogs. These certificates can be obtained from the USDA office in your state.

Note: The process to receive a PETS certificate should be started at a minimum of seven months before the expected travel date.

Requirements of PETS:

1. An accredited veterinarian must certify the identification of the pet, the pet's rabies inoculation, and the results of rabies testing. The PETS certificate bearing the Veterinary Services (VS) logo, available to accredited veterinarians through the federal Veterinary Services offices, is the only certificate that can be used. (See resources, page 199, for more information.)

2. Only microchip-identified animals will qualify for entry. The accredited veterinarian must certify that she verified the chip number. UK port officials can read microchips conforming to ISO Standard 11784 or Annex A to ISO Standard 11785. If other chips are used, owners will be obliged to present the proper working chip reader to the port inspector on arrival in the United Kingdom.

3. A licensed veterinarian using an approved-labeled vaccine must properly inoculate the microchip-identified animal against rabies.

4. After rabies inoculation (an interval of thirty days is suggested), the microchip-identified animal must have a blood sample to confirm that vaccination was successful. The Veterinary Diagnostic Laboratory, at Kansas State University, in Manhattan, Kansas, is the laboratory of choice for nonmilitary United States and Canadian pet owners. The certifying veterinarian will confirm microchip identification at the time the blood sample is collected.

5. Once the laboratory verifies that the microchip-identified animal has a satisfactory level of antibodies against rabies of at least 0.5 International Units per milliliter, the accredited veterinarian may issue the PETS Certificate. The microchip identification will be verified at the time the certificate is issued. The PETS Certificate will indicate the period of validity, starting six months after the date the rabies blood test was drawn and ending on the expiration date of the rabies vaccination. Certificates can then be reissued so long as the rabies vaccinations are updated before expiration, and the replacement certificate will again be valid as long as vaccination is current.

6. In addition to the PETS Certificate, between twenty-four and forty-eight hours before being checked in for departure, the pet must be presented to a licensed, practicing veterinarian who will read and verify the microchip number, treat the animals for ticks and tapeworms, using approved products, and issue the Certificate of Tick and Tapeworm Treatment. Both the PETS Certificate and the Treatment Certificate must accompany the pet to the UK.

7. PETS allows entry to the UK for those animals originating or residing in approved European Union (EU) and Non-EU countries. The DEFRA Animal Health and Welfare site (http://defra.gov.uk) lists approved countries. (Note: These charts are updated on a regular basis and should be reviewed before you make travel arrangements.)

Traveling with Your Pet to the British Isles

United Kingdom-resident dogs, cats, and ferrets can travel to any of the European Union (EU) countries and return to the UK under the Pet Travel Scheme (PETS). Pets that come from any of these countries can also enter the UK under PETS as long as they meet the standards. Pets must not have been outside any of the EU or non-EU listed countries in the six calendar months before traveling to the United Kingdom. Pets that reside in the Channel Islands, the Isle of Man, or the Republic of Ireland can reenter the UK under PETS from any qualifying country if they meet the rules.

Pets that have first entered the British Isles under the Scheme can then travel between the United Kingdom, the Channel Islands, the Isle of Man, and the Republic of Ireland without the need for extra documentation. But you should always take your pet's documents with you in the event you must present them. Owners of pets entering the Channel Islands or the Republic of Ireland from outside the British Isles should contact the appropriate authorities for advice on approved routes and any other requirements.

Dogs, cats, and ferrets prepared for PETS in, or returning under PETS to, the United Kingdom from the Republic of Cyprus may enter or re-enter the UK without quarantine. But PETS-compliant animals traveling from north Cyprus (the area north of the Buffer Zone) or from St. Bartholomew or St. Martin (the French part of the island) must be licensed into quarantine for six months on arrival in the United

no pet left behind international travel

Kingdom. This must be arranged before the animal travels. Contact the PETS Helpline (44 (0)870 241 1710) to check for any change in this situation.

Pet Policies for Non-European Union Countries

Ferrets can, having traveled to any of the non-EU countries or territories, return to the UK under the Scheme. Pets that come from any of these countries can also enter the UK under PETS as long as they meet the rules. Pets can enter the UK via any other EU or non-EU listed country. But pets must not have been outside any of the EU or non-EU listed countries in the six calendar months before traveling to the United Kingdom.

The maximum number of all types of pet animals each person may bring into the EU from most non-EU listed countries is five. But this rule does not apply to animals brought from Andorra, Iceland, Liechtenstein, Monaco, Norway, San Marino, Switzerland, or the Vatican.

Pets traveling on a sea crossing or by rail into the United Kingdom must accompany passengers in a vehicle. Certain routes allow only guide/hearing dogs. Of course, routes may change and new ones may be added, and some routes are seasonal or irregular, so it is best to check availability with the transport company before booking your trip to the United Kingdom.

Pets and the Eurotunnel

When you book your trip, notify Eurotunnel that an animal will be carried. Animals must remain in your vehicle (unless authorized to leave the vehicle by Eurotunnel), and you must keep them under your control at all times. Cats must be transported in a basket or suitable container capable of being securely closed.

When you arrive in France, you must present your pet and all of his documents to the Eurotunnel staff at the terminal's "Pets Control Point."

A flowchart of the owner's procedure, an outline of the procedure, veterinarian information, a sample PETS Entry or Re-entry Certificate, and the certification of treatment against ticks and tapeworms form may be obtained by visiting the Department for Environmental Food and Affairs (DEFRA) Web site (http://defra.gov.uk). It is always a good idea to check this Web site when planning a trip to Europe with your pet, to ensure that you have the latest information regarding PETS, quarantines, and restrictions.

It is also wise to check the Web sites for the other federal agencies that have a role in the import/export of animals: the United States Centers for Disease Control and Prevention (www.cdc.gov/) and the United States Customs Service (www.cbp.gov/).

Be warned: Eurotunnel may refuse to transport your pet if they deem him unfit for travel or consider him to represent a danger or nuisance to other travelers or to Eurotunnel staff. If your pet is unfit to travel on a shuttle or does not comply with the requirements of PETS, you will have to make arrangements for importing the animal into the United Kingdom under quarantine regulations, and you will be responsible for any quarantine and other costs, as well as all costs arising from any delay. Tickets for animals are nonrefundable.

Importing Pets into Canada

Pet, show, and service dogs need proof only of receiving a rabies vaccination within the three years before their export to Canada. This proof can take the form of a rabies vaccination certificate, or the vaccination can be documented on the health certificate, if a health certificate is required. The only signature required is that of the licensed or accredited veterinarian. All puppies will be examined by a Canadian Agriculture Inspector at the first port of entry. A copy of the Canadian Veterinary Health Certificate can be downloaded from the Agriculture Canada Web site (www.inspection.gc.ca/english/anima/heasan/export/exporte.shtml). Dogs entering Canada from the United States that qualify for admission with a rabies certificate include:

• Any dog greater than eight months of age

• An assistance dog that is certified as a guide, hearing, or service dog—if the person accompanying the dog to Canada is also the dog's user

• Any dog exported on a temporary basis for competition in a show or trial, if at the time of importation proof of entry in a show or trial is provided

No more than two pet dogs can be accompanied by their owner into Canada.

Cats

Pet and show cats must be accompanied by a rabies vaccination certificate issued by a licensed veterinarian clearly identifying the animal and showing that she was vaccinated against rabies during the three years immediately preceding importation into Canada. This requirement does not apply to a kitten that is apparently younger than three months.

Birds

For import purposes, the expression "pet bird" means a personally owned and cared-for bird. It applies only to species commonly known as "caged" birds—birds in the parrot family, songbirds such as canaries and finches, and similarly common pet birds. The expression does not apply to pigeons, doves, species of wild or domesticated fowl, or game birds. The necessary certification to clear Customs will be made by completing a form, which is available at Customs. Under that arrangement, no import permit or quarantine period is required. If these conditions cannot be met, it will be necessary for you to obtain an import permit from the appropriate Canadian Food Inspection Agency regional office in the province to which you will be traveling. The importation of birds into Canada is also subject to the control of the Canadian Wildlife Service

Extra Info

Absorbent Liners

Spilled food or water—or stress, layovers, and too much to drink—can all result in a messy crate and an uncomfortable environment for your pet. I recommend that you travel with two or three washable carrier liners, in case you need to freshen the carrier. Sherpa® packages three sizes of washable faux lambskin pads in inexpensive three-packs (www.sherpapet.com/ products/).

(Convention on International Trade in Endangered Species (CITES)). You may contact them by telephone at 613-997-1840 or fax at 614-953-6283.

Personally owned pet birds can be imported into Canada under the following conditions:

- The birds must accompany the owner or be in the possession of an immediate family member.
- The birds must be found to be healthy when inspected at the port of entry.
- The owner must sign a declaration stating that the birds have been in the owner's possession for the ninety-day period preceding the date of importation and have not been in contact with any other birds during that time.
- The owner must sign a declaration stating that the birds are the owner's personal pets and are not being imported for the purpose of resale.
- The owner or any member of the family must not have imported birds into Canada under this pet bird provision during the preceding ninety-day period.

Exotic Pet Travelers

Dogs and cats are not the only pets that travel with their owners. Owners of birds, reptiles, rabbits, ferrets, hamsters, and other small pets travel with their best friends, too. As pet species vary, however, so do rules, so begin your research in the early planning stages of your trip if you want to be accompanied by a more exotic pet than a cat or dog.

For information about importing into Canada such pets as amphibians and reptiles, birds from countries other than the United States, fish, foxes, skunks, raccoons, ferrets, rodents, horses (from the United States), pet primates, scorpions, or spiders, visit www.inspection.gc.ca/english/anima/heasan/import/petse.shtml.

If the animal you wish to import is not listed at that site, refer to the Automated Import Reference System (AIRS), which provides information about import requirements for all commodities regulated by the Canadian Food Inspection Agency. You'll find links to AIRS on the above Web site.

The Canadian Food Inspection Agency (CFIA) provides additional pet information (phone: 613-225-2342; www.inspection.gc.ca). If you need assistance while in Canada, contact the United States Embassy at 490 Sussex Drive, Ottawa, ON, Canada K1N 1G8; phone: 613-238-5335.

Importing Birds into Foreign Countries

All birds—those taken out of the country, as well as those being returned—are subject to United States Customs Pets and Wildlife Licensing and Health Requirements. In addition, nearly all birds coming into the country require a permit from the United States Fish and Wildlife Service. To prevent the introduction of exotic poultry diseases into the United States, the United States Department of Agriculture regulates the importation of all birds.

Most birds must be quarantined upon arrival for a minimum of thirty days in a USDA Animal Import Center (New York City, Miami, or Los Angeles). Quarantine space must be reserved in advance by contacting one of the USDA Animal Import Centers. All quarantine fees must be paid in full in advance. A USDA import permit is required for most imported birds. Permit application forms can be obtained by contacting the USDA Animal Import Center directly or can be found on the USDA Web site at www.aphis.usda.gov.

Birds imported into the United States must be inspected by a USDA port veterinarian at the first United States port of entry. This inspection must be arranged by contacting the port veterinarian at least seventy-two hours before travel. A current veterinary health certificate must accompany the bird. The health certificate must be endorsed by a national veterinarian of the country of export and be issued within thirty days of importation.

no pet left behind international travel

Tips for traveling in a plane with a bird:

- Provide dry and moist food, along with leafy foods and fresh fruit, instead of water during the flight. (Pet shops sell a dried sponge-cake type of bird food that can be soaked in water.)
- Clip your bird's wings before taking it on a trip (see page 85) — it takes only one flight to lose a pet forever, but feathers will grow back.
- Bring toys for your bird, but not anything sharp that could cause injury during turbulence.
- Have a cover for the cage or carrier to reduce stimulation and drafts, and to create a sense of security.

Birds returning to the United States may be quarantined in the owner's home for a minimum of thirty days. To show proof of United States origin, the birds must be accompanied by a veterinary health certificate issued by a United States veterinarian before leaving the country.

Birds imported from Canada are exempt from quarantine requirements. But all birds must be examined by a USDA port veterinarian at the first United States port of entry. If the birds enter the United States via a United States-Canadian land border port, no import permit is required. If the birds enter via an airport, an import permit is required (for the permit application, visit www.aphis.usda.gov).

Importing Pet Rabbits

Domestic or pet rabbits imported from the United States must be presented to Canada Border Services Agency staff upon entry. The importation of pet rabbits does not require import permits or health certificates. Canada has both permit and quarantine requirements for the importation of domestic rabbits from countries other than the United States. To obtain detailed information about this process, you should contact the Canadian Food Inspection Agency (CFIA) office in the province into which the rabbits will be imported. You will be required to complete and submit an Application for Permit to Import to the CFIA. You will also need a signed declaration that the rabbits have been in your possession as personally owned pets and that you will personally accompany the rabbits from the country of origin to Canada. You should apply for the import permit at least thirty days in advance of your proposed importation. You will be told how much your fees will be when applying for an import permit, approval of a quarantine facility, and inspection of animals. Contact the Canadian Wildlife Service at www.cws-scf.ec.gc.ca or by phone 613-997-1840. Call 819-953-6283 to determine whether the rabbits you wish to import require CITES import permits.

Pet Travel to Mexico

Taking your pet to Mexico with you is a straightforward affair. Pets must be accompanied by a Health Certificate issued by a licensed veterinarian. Health certificates for personal pets do not need to be endorsed by a Veterinary Services veterinarian. The animals must be inoculated against rabies (unless younger than four months old) and distemper (dates of vaccination must appear on the health certificate). The health certificate must be in duplicate and bear the name and address of the owner, along with a description of the animal (species, age, sex), and state that the animal has been examined and found free of any contagious disease.

To return to the United States from Mexico with a dog requires nothing more than proof of a rabies vaccination. But when returning from Mexico, a bird purchased there may be quarantined for six months. For more information, see the United States Department of State Tips for Travelers to Mexico at www.travel .state.gov. Birds who originated in the United States but are returning from Mexico may be quarantined in the owner's home for a minimum of thirty days. For you to show proof of United States origin, the birds must be accompanied by a veterinary

no pet left behind international travel

health certificate issued by a United States veterinarian before you leave the United States with your pet.

Troubleshooting

Because of such high traffic in parrot smuggling, it is crucial that you have all your bird's paperwork in order—to protect both you and your pet. This is especially critical while traveling through states bordering Mexico. I recommend that you carry a portfolio containing copies of proof of ownership, sales receipts, your breeder's name and address, and medical records. This information could be invaluable, especially if an emergency occurs.

Pet ferrets traveling with owners to Mexico must be accompanied by a Health Certificate issued by a licensed veterinarian and endorsed by a Veterinary Services veterinarian. It should contain the name and address of the owner and certification statements verifying that the animals were examined and found to be free of any clinical evidence of infectious or contagious diseases and of ectoparasites. If your pet dies or becomes ill within thirty days of entry into Mexico, you must notify the Division of Animal Health.

For Import Health Requirements of Mexico for pet ornamental and songbirds from the United States, contact the Mexican embassy (see resources, page 193).

Popular Island Vacation Destinations

You don't have to leave your furry or feathered family members behind next time you want a vacation of sand, surf, and tropical delights. You and your pet can enjoy a no-hassle, fabulous vacation in the Bahamas, soaking up the sun and dancing in the moon's soft glow.

To find a place to stay, you might visit www.caribbeanplacestostay.com. The site offers a list of pet-friendly rental vacation villas, condos, and homes. You'll deal directly with homeowners who are understanding of your needs and very helpful. You can travel to the Bahamas on a chartered boat, but if you are in a hurry to get your feet (or paws) in the sand, air travel may be the better option.

An import permit is required to bring any animal into the Bahamas. This permit is available at www.bahamas.com or by mail: Director, Department of Agriculture, P.O. Box N—3704, Nassau, Bahamas; phone: 242-325-7502. There is a $10 processing fee. For the United States and Canada, the following are the main provisions of the import permit as it applies to dogs and cats:

- Must be at least six months of age
- Must be accompanied by a valid certificate that substantiates the pet has been vaccinated against rabies within not less than one month and not more than ten months before importation
- Must be accompanied by a Veterinary Health Certificate presented within forty-eight hours of arrival in the Commonwealth of the Bahamas to a licensed veterinarian for an examination.

Pets Bound for Puerto Rico

The beaches of Puerto Rico are all open to the public and their pets. My friend Dr. Helen Asquine Fazio and Raja, her shih-tzu, enjoy feeling the sand between their toes on the island's northwest coast. Helen warns, however, that Raja does not particularly enjoy the island's enormous iguanas that share the waters. Always keep a close eye on your pets when in a natural environment. A seemingly peaceful setting can turn dangerous in a matter of seconds for a small pet with a curious disposition.

No passport or visa is necessary for United States citizens traveling into or out of Puerto Rico, but if you decide to bring your pet, you must have a rabies quarantine certificate from a veterinarian stating that your pet has had a rabies shot. For more information, contact the United States Department of Agriculture Puerto Rico office, Veterinary Division, at 787-766-6050.

the best
places
tr

to
avel
with your pet

Going on a vacation shouldn't include distressed whimpers, distraught meows, ruffled feathers, or sad, soulful eyes that send you on a guilt trip before you even walk out the door. Vacation should be a time to kick back and be carefree, but how can you be carefree knowing that your best friend is "ruffing" it at the neighborhood kennel? Let's face it, when your favorite furry, feathered, or even finned friend isn't by your side, vacations just feel incomplete, like someone important is missing.

no pet left behind best places

Traveling with your pet can be a fun-filled bonding experience and the places you can travel with your pet are practically limitless. In this chapter, I'll help you focus on the fun of traveling with your pet by helping you find the best pet-friendly locations and lodgings both at home and abroad—including some Sherpa-approved favorites. Whether you want to take your best friend with you on a holiday of skiing, shopping, communing with nature, or casino hopping, you'll find plenty of sources and practical advice here.

Pet Lodgings
Where Will Both of You Have the Most Fun?

Pets are part of your family, so it is only natural to want to bring them along on your family vacations. And who's to say you can't? Explore the gambit of pet holidays, from big-city hotels and shopping districts to rustic campgrounds, special dog camps, and even boating and hiking adventures that you can share with your best friend.

Hotels

Gone are the days when you had to spend hours on the phone trying to locate a comfortable hotel that would accept your pet. Now you can just look online, where you'll find some great pet-oriented travel sites that use the same databases as major travel agencies. (See resources, page 182.) These sites simplify your search by extracting and listing the best pet-friendly hotels here and abroad. Pet-friendly hotels actually sometimes compete, offering both discounts and people-friendly amenities, such as family discounts and nonsmoking and handicap-accessible rooms to lure travelers with pet in tow.

Some hotels offer truly luxurious pet accommodations, such as a pet room-service menu with a choice of pet foods, bowls, vitamins, toys, and blankets for your pet. Many also offer a cat-visiting or dog-walking service, pet day care, and in-hotel grooming.

Keep in mind that traveling with a pet is a privilege, and a destructive or disagreeable pet can wear out his welcome even at a pet-welcoming hotel. Good hotel petiquette includes calling ahead to make reservations and asking whether there are any restrictions as to animal size, age, or the number of pets accepted. For more on hotel petiquette, see page 56.

For more on hotel petiquette, see page 56.

Motels for People and Pets

Statistics show that active, mobile seniors routinely travel by car with their pets, which may have fueled the demand for pet-friendly motel rooms.

Motel chains are conveniently positioned along major auto routes; staying at motels of the same chain during a trip can offer a reassuringly familiar quality of life off the road as you drive from one town to another. Best of all, most motels have grassy areas and reserve a few pet-friendly rooms on the ground floor near an outside door to expedite dog-walking. Because there are usually a limited number of pet rooms per unit, be sure to trace your route and reserve yours at least twenty-four hours ahead of your estimated arrival time.

As a bonus, most chain motels these days are not only located near carry-out food chains, where you can take your pet to the drive-thru window with you, but also usually near shopping centers, which are sure to include a pet shop and supermarket where you can stock up on pet food, toys, bedding, and other essentials. For a complete list of pet-friendly motels, see *Traveling with Your Pet, 9th edition: The AAA Pet Book,* published by the Automobile Association of America (AAA), which is available in bookstores across the country.

Lodgings Just for Pets

What do you do with your best friend if, after reaching your destination, you want to take a no-pets-allowed day trip, such as whale-watching or a local bus tour? There is no need to leave your pet behind in an empty hotel room or consign him to a strange kennel. Instead, your pet can enjoy his own activity-filled day at a pet hotel or day camp. The national pet store chain PetCo now operates pet hotels and doggie day camps in half of the states. There your dog can have a real carpeted room with a bed, and cats have rooms with picture windows that look out over the pet hotel. Day camps offer a playground and group play time. The pet hotel has staff to care for your pet around the clock, seven days a week. For both hotel and day camp, veterinarians are available at all times and they even provide grooming. Security cameras and special identification collars ensure that your pet is safe, and you can even call and talk to your pet on the telephone.

Other facilities, such as the Texas-based chain Pappy's Pet Lodge, also offer obedience classes and a spa, where pets can be lavishly bathed and groomed. Pappy's caters to all pets, including ferrets, birds, and rodents. Because pet hotels, day camps, and spas are less numerous than kennels and pet-friendly hotels, your best bet is to find one at your destination.

Resorts

The Travel Industry Association states that one in ten American families travel with a pet, and dogs are the most common traveling pet. Not surprisingly, dogs are the most catered-to pet at resorts and spas. When resorts come to my mind, skiing is at the top of the list. One of the country's oldest ski resort towns, Sun Valley, is also called the most pet-friendly resort in the country. It starts with the town because, in the old days, sled dogs were essential to survival. Today most households have a dog, and hiking with dogs is a popular pastime. Most restaurants in town have carry-out windows or

no pet left behind best places

sidewalk café seats for the pets' convenience. Most resorts in Sun Valley cater to pets, and there are doggie day care facilities that offer exercise classes and massages. The town positions water bowls at street intersections, and many stores are pet-friendly.

At the famous Escondido, California, Wyndham Peaks Resort & Golden Door Spa, human guests can share the spa treatment with their dogs. Guestrooms have adjustable food and water bowls for different-sized dogs and feature plush doggie beds. In the dog-friendly wet treatment room, licensed therapists treat canines to a twenty-five-minute massage. Before departure, guests can visit the canine consignment boutique to purchase reminders of their stays, including fleece sweaters, mittens, fancy leashes, collars, and toys; spa robes can be custom-made for pooches. The resort offers access to 250 hiking trails and a river. The entire town is geared toward pedestrians and has designated "puppy parking" areas, as well as special cars for pets on the free gondola. For contact information and listings for these and other pet-friendly spas, visit www.spaindex.com/Lifestyles/petfriendly.htm.

RV Parks, Campgrounds, and Dog Camps

According to Jack and Julee Meltzer, authors of *Camping and RVing with Dogs*, 30 million families take their dogs camping each year. There are literally thousands of campgrounds that allow pets. Still, although you are in the great outdoors, there may be places within the campgrounds that pets are not allowed to go—swimming pools and certain camping cabins, for example. Also keep in mind that some campgrounds have

no pet left behind best places

breed restrictions as well as a restriction on the number of pets one family can bring into the camp. Some places may also request a rabies vaccination certificate, so before you head out to your favorite campsite, make sure to contact them and get all of the information you need. For a list of campgrounds, check the most current version of *Trailer Life RV Parks, Campgrounds and Service Directory* by Trailer Life Enterprises.

Dog Camps

Dog camps are often an excellent way for you and your pooch to share new adventures, such as herding, tracking, nature walks, campfires with s'mores, and storytelling. Some are intended to be weekend or longer vacations where you and your pet can learn new things and explore a variety of new activities in a relaxing atmosphere. Others cater to people who want pet obedience classes or pet-assisted therapy certification, or who are competing in a dog sport like rally, freestyle, fly ball, or agility and want to improve their skills.

Perhaps the most well known of the dog camps is Camp Gone to the Dogs. This Vermont camp offers a week-long session with introductions to fly ball, herding, agility, clicker training, canine nutrition, and more. Another, Dog Scout Camp, has this unique motto: "Let us learn new things that we may become more helpful." Unlike other dog camps that are

Troubleshooting

Do not let a run-in between your pet and a wad of bubble gum or some other minor mishap ruin your vacation. Try these quick fixes:

Chewing gum: Try icing the gum for a minimum of ten minutes to make it more manageable and easy to remove from fur or feathers. You can also use peanut butter. Apply the peanut butter to the gum; the peanut oil will loosen the gum. After about twenty minutes, you can carefully work the gum out of the hair. (This works best when applied where your pet can't reach the peanut butter, which is a favorite treat for many pets.)

Burrs: Soften the burrs with vegetable or baby oil, and then carefully work them out of fur. If the burrs are not near your pet's face, it may be helpful to slip a kitchen fork or something similar under the burr to help remove it.

Tar: Try soaking the tarred area in vegetable or baby oil. Leave the oil on for an hour or more, and then bathe your dog or cat. The oil should cause the tar to slide off the hair shaft. Since this method can be messy, shampoo with a strong shampoo (or even dishwashing soap) to remove the oil. If any oil remains, apply baby powder or cornstarch to the oily area. Leave it on for twenty minutes, and then wash again with dishwashing soap. Follow with a pet shampoo to restore the pH balance of your pet's skin and fur.

primarily about recreation, Dog Scout Camp tries to teach your dog skills that will serve her in real life. It also teaches owners how to better communicate with their dogs. Just like boy and girl scouts, dog scouts earn merit badges in activities such as obedience, backpacking, and water safety. Owners will also gain insight into how dogs learn and how they can help their dog become a better pet. The camp, located in St. Helen, Michigan, in the northern Lower Peninsula, is rustic but beautiful. There's a lake for swimming and boating, and many miles of hiking trails. For a complete listing of dog camps in this country and Canada, see resources, pages 177–179.

Did You Know?

Happiness is a swim! But if your campground or park does not allow your pet to swim in the same place you do, take along a lightweight plastic kiddy pool when camping so that your best friend can take a cool dip on a hot day.

Condos, Time-Shares, Cabins, and Other Rentals

Perhaps the closest thing to home you and your pet can experience are vacation rentals, whether condos, time-shares, or cabins. You can find them in all the most popular vacation spots from East and West Coast beach rentals to lakeside getaways, golf course resorts, and mountain ski rentals. If you are adventurous enough to try trading houses, you can vacation in far-flung places such as Hawaii, England, France, or Germany with little investment. Just be sure to discuss your pet with the owner in advance because most of these rentals have very strict pet size limits, and they may welcome one species and reject others. Also be prepared to leave a sizable damage deposit and to pay an extra, reasonable daily fee for your pet. For information on finding pet-friendly time-shares and condos, see resources, page 182.

Eating Out

In Europe, dogs are welcome nearly everywhere, including restaurants. American restaurants, however, hindered by health codes, have had a harder time of it, usually

restricting pets to their outdoor seating areas. But lately some interesting innovations in dining, such as special pet seating areas and even all-pet restaurants and bakeries, have opened more avenues to traveling pets. The easiest way to find pet-friendly eateries where you're staying is to ask the hotel desk, dog camp, or fellow travelers who have been there before.

Puttin' on the Dog

Do you long to dine with your dog at a fancy restaurant where she can nosh from a plate and golden charger set on a damask tablecloth? In certain places your dream can be a reality. The Dining Dog Café and Bakery of Edmonds, Washington, offers a complete menu of doggie cocktails, appetizers, entrées, and desserts. They provide a people menu, as well. This restaurant is also available for special events and private parties. Café J in San Francisco (415-970-2208) offers biscuits to canine guests, while Bridge's Café, in Portland, Oregon, provides water bowls. In Chicago, Cucina Bella Trattoria and its sister restaurant, Cucina Bella Osteria, have "Doggie Dining" seating areas and offer special pastas and treats for pooch guests. Offerings at Park Bench Café in Huntington Beach, California, include "Hot Diggity Dog," a beef hot dog cut into bite-sized pieces; the "Wrangler Roundup," a ground-turkey patty; and "Chilly Paws," a scoop of vanilla ice cream. The Three Dog Bakery, which first welcomed pets into its small shop in the tony Kansas City Plaza, began making treats and dog food from people-quality ingredients in the 1980s and now has franchises in nineteen states, Canada, and Japan.

But what if you don't happen to be near one of these ritzy canine eateries while traveling? Most of the time, you can find a local restaurant, café, or ice cream shop with outdoor seating that will welcome a well-behaved pet. If you are on the highway, fast-food restaurants with drive-thru windows are your best option. But if you are hungry and neither of these is available, your next best option is to order carry-out food from a restaurant, pizza shop, or grocery deli counter.

Parks

Nearly all metro areas have multiple public parks that welcome pets. Many people visit these parks, so observing good petiquette is essential. Most parks require that you keep your pet on a six- or eight-foot leash and that you pick up after her. Some parks, such as the City of San Diego Park and Recreation Department, reserve some trails or beaches where you can let your pet run off-leash. For the protection of a puppy, do not take her to a public park until she has had all of her vaccinations.

Dog Parks

Whether you live in Charlotte, North Carolina, or Phoenix, Arizona, you can find metropolitan dog parks. These relatively new and wonderful innovations are fenced parks designed especially for the enjoyment of dogs. Dogs can run off-leash and play with other dogs, swim, play games, and run obstacle courses. No matter where you are staying on vacation, you are usually within a fifteen-minute drive of a dog park. Check with your hotel office or the internet to find one because these parks may give your dog a chance to socialize with other dogs and may give him the only opportunity during your vacation to run without being confined to a leash.

National and State Parks, Wildlife, and Privately Controlled Areas

National parks are some of the most visited destination spots in the United States for vacation travelers. Every year, millions

When you do take your dog to a sit-down dinner at a sidewalk cafe or restaurant that caters to dogs, you'll want him to be on his best behavior. This short list of table manners will make him a welcome guest at any eatery.

- Keep your dog on a short leash tied to your chair so that he won't wander off or trip the waiters.
- Teach your dog to sit or lie by your side while you are eating. Practice this on a regular basis before taking him to a restaurant.
- If a waiter brings a bowl of water or food to your dog, tip generously for the extra service.
- Bring a special treat, such as a hollow nylon toy filled with cream cheese or peanut butter, so that he'll stay focused and busy while you eat.
- If your dog won't settle down, take him on a short walk to calm him down before returning to your table.

of people visit their favorite national parks. But have you ever tried to bring your best friend along? The majority of national parks are not very welcoming to pets.

Fortunately, there are at least some dog-friendly national forests. An excellent site that will help you find tail-friendly trails throughout the United States is www.hikewithyourdog.com.

The general policy for national parks is that dogs must be on a six-foot or shorter leash at all times. Most of the parks allow dogs in campgrounds and in developed areas, which include parking lots, your car, or within fifty to one hundred feet of the road. The majority of national parks do not allow dogs on any hiking, walking, or backcountry trails, on beaches, or inside buildings. A few lesser-known national parks do not allow you even to drive into the park if you have a pet in your car.

Some national parks have exceptions to these stringent pet rules. Parks including the Grand Canyon National Park and Acadia National Park allow dogs on some trails and are well worth a visit. For the majority of national parks that do not allow dogs on any trails, a fair amount of sightseeing can still be done. Keep in mind that the majority of visitors to national parks do not venture too far from their cars. This means that there are typically many sites and points of interest to see right from the comfort of your own car.

So how much can you really see at our national parks when bringing your pet along? See resources, page 177 for a list of the top five pet-friendly national parks from the National Park Service.

For people who actually want to go on a long wilderness hike with their dog, more dog-friendly national forests are usually adjacent to or located nearby national parks. In the same vein, state parks and wildlife areas can be more open to hiking with dogs although most have strict leash requirements, and some, such as Virginia's state parks,

Even if you've never been a boy or girl scout, you must be prepared when exploring nature with your best friend. Here are some important treatments and remedies to know and remember:

Insect bites and stings: Use ice to reduce the swelling. For quick relief from a wasp or bee sting, dab the spot with plain vinegar and then apply baking soda. If you do not have vinegar or baking soda, a small mud pie placed over the bite or sting will ease the pain and swelling. If your pet has been stung in the mouth, immediately seek veterinary assistance—swelling can close the throat.

Snakebites: Prompt medical attention (within two hours if at all possible) is key. Immediately immobilize the bitten area, and pay attention to these "don'ts":

- Do not allow your pet to walk because the more your pet moves, the faster the venom will spread.
- Do not apply ice to the bite—venom constricts the blood vessels and ice only compounds the constriction.
- Do not try to clean the bite.

• Do not use a tourniquet—the body's natural immune system fights off the venom. Cutting off the blood flow will either minimize or eliminate the body's natural defenses.

Poison ivy or oak: While poison ivy or oak will not bother your pet, the poison can be passed to you. If you know your pet has come into contact with one of these poisons, use rubber gloves when handling him. Wash him in salt water, and follow with a clear water rinse. Then shampoo with a mild soap and rinse again.

Skunks: If a skunk should appear on the scene, try to keep your pet quiet and do not attempt to scare the skunk away—just back off and leave as quickly and quietly as possible. But if the skunk has done his deed and your pet was unfortunately on the receiving end of the spray, these remedies should help:
• Saturate your pet's fur with tomato juice. Let the fur dry and then brush it out and shampoo.
• Combine 1 quart of 3 percent hydrogen peroxide and $1/_4$ cup baking soda with a short shot of liquid soap. Let the solution soak on your pet's fur for fifteen minutes; then rinse with clear water, shampoo, and rinse again.
• Combine 5 parts water with 1 part vinegar. Let the solution soak on your pet's fur for fifteen minutes; then rinse with clear water, shampoo, and rinse again.

Ticks: Soak with lighter fluid or rubbing alcohol to loosen, and then gently tweeze the tick out, making sure you have removed the head.

When hiking, a wet bandana wrapped around your dog's neck will keep him cool and comfortable. It's a good idea for humans, as well!

which have a rabies alert, require proof of rabies vaccination. Beaches, visitor centers, and other buildings are usually off-limits to four-footed friends.

Privately Controlled Areas, such as land owned by a water company or land conservation nonprofits, and endowed arboretums, botanical gardens, and living history museums are often open to the public. A surprising number of them allow pets on leashes, and some, such as the colonial home and farm of James Madison in Virginia, even have courtesy kennels where pets can temporarily relax while their owners tour the former President's house.

Tours

A guided tour is often the best way to get a general idea of your destination or to gain admission to a private museum or other hard-to-enter location. Pet travelers, take heart: Many tour companies allow pets on board. As with other activities, call ahead to make sure your pet will be accepted, and be sure to ask about any special rules or restrictions. Carry a canteen and water bowl, along with some treats, to keep your pet hydrated and energized as you beat the pavement. PetsOnTheGo.com lists the following among its most popular pet-friendly tours:

- Chartered boat tours of Boston Harbor and San Francisco Bay
- A ski-gondola ride at Wildcat or Telluride, combined with a hike down the mountain
- A train ride through the redwood forests on California's Skunk Train
- Walking tours in Washington, DC

Beaches

While many dogs love to feel the sand and surf on their paws, not every beach is welcoming to our canine friends. The good news is that there are approximately two hundred dog-friendly coastal beaches in the United States. Many beaches in heavily populated areas such as Miami and Los Angeles do not allow pets because too many people have ignored leash laws and pooper scooper laws, leading to conflicts on the beach. To avoid disappointment, be sure to check whether pets are allowed on the beach that is in your vacation agenda. If they are, find out during what times they are welcome and whether they are required to wear a leash.

When you pack a beach bag for your best friend, include:

- A towel for drying your wet dog
- Drinking water and a bowl
- Your doggy first-aid kit
- Pick-up bags
- A floating fetch toy
- A life jacket, if the water is rough or your dog is not an expert swimmer
- Sunscreen, for dogs with light skin/short fur and pink noses (look for baby-safe, PABA-free, hypoallergenic types of sunscreen)

Respect all leash laws on the beach, and be courteous to fellow beachgoers. This means that if your dog takes a dip, do not permit him to shake off water in the vicinity of an unsuspecting sunbather. If you have a social dog who wants to visit another dog or beachgoer, make sure he's welcome. And always scoop your pet's poop.

During crowded summer months, it's best to visit the beach early in the day or at twilight when the crowds have thinned out. If you discover a beach where pets do not have to be leashed, make sure your dog responds to your verbal commands.

Lake Adventures with Pets

Whether water-skiing, fishing, or just hanging out on a pontoon boat, spending a day at the lake is a fun activity for you and your dog—less so for cats, who universally detest water, and for smaller cage-bound pets, who would find little enjoyment in the constant rocking of a boat. These landlubbers are best left in the comfort of a hotel room or pet day care while you spend a day at the lake. But most dogs just love a day at the lake, and some can even be taught to wakeboard behind a boat.

But before heading to the water, make sure you have your dog's comfort and safety needs in hand. All dogs should wear a life jacket when in a boat. Not all dogs can swim, and those who do are not always good at it. You can buy a flotation vest for a dog at any water-sports store or in sporting-goods stores. Most of these have a practical handle on the back to help you lift your dog out of the water. If your dog falls overboard without a life jacket, she could quickly become exhausted paddling or experience hypothermia (see page 65 for symptoms and treatment).

Start with the skier's "Rule of 100": When the air temperature plus the water temperature equals 100°F, the water is warm enough for swimming or skiing. Pack a towel for your dog, along with a water-resistant synthetic sweater or fleecy shirt in case he appears to be chilly or shivering. Take fresh drinking water, and if the boat is pitching, squirt water into your dog's mouth from a sports bottle.

If you intend to go fishing, be extremely careful to keep hooks out of the reach of your pet, and consider using barbless hooks—in the unhappy event that your pet is hooked, these are less painful to extract than barbed hooks. See page 80 for a list of first-aid items to take along.

If your dog has never gone boating, acquaint him with the boat while it is parked on the shore. Allow periodic lakeside potty breaks, or be prepared to pick up after your pet on the boat.

Lake Destinations

Dogs have accompanied their owners into lakeland wilderness areas to enjoy hiking, hunting, and boating ever since colonial days. This strong tradition of lakes and dogs lives on at such rustic lake resorts as The Point and Lake Placid Lodge on Lake Placid

in the Adirondack Mountains of Upstate New York. Rocky Hollow lakeside cabins and cottages on Bull Shoals Lake in the picturesque Ozark Mountains of Arkansas, where you can boat and fish for trout by day and then gather around a campfire in the evening, is another dog-friendly resort. Less than two hours from Los Angeles is Big Bear Lake, a rustic lake area where dogs are welcome on rental boats and where you can explore lakeside trails together. Be sure to call ahead to reserve pet-friendly lake cabins or rooms and boats, which can be limited in number. Check to see whether there are restrictions, such as a "no-puppy" rule.

Mountain Areas

From misty morning strolls in the Adirondacks of New York or the Blue Ridge Mountains of North Carolina to fishing trout streams in the piney mountains around Scottsdale, Arizona, to a dog-friendly ski-gondola ride at Wildcat or Telluride, the mountains are definitely pet-friendly. Chances are you'll be more interested in hiking, biking, or boating with your dog than other types of pets, and many resorts and cabins welcome canine family members.

Because there may be free-roaming moose, elk, deer, coyotes, wildcats, and bears in the mountains, dogs should be leashed to avoid an unpleasant encounter, especially when exploring some of the mountain trails. And again, be respectful of nature and your fellow hikers, and always look for, and use, the biodegradable "Pet Pickup" bags in rustic wooden dispensers, conveniently situated along many trails.

Chartering Your Own Boat

SHERPA CRUISE LINE

Even though SuNae and I much prefer the air "waves" to the ones in a lake or the ocean, I have put together a list of bare boat, crewed charter, and cruising options for seafaring pet lovers. These options range from simple bare boats and skippered charters to lavish multimillion-dollar vessels with a crew. The following is a general overview of what many charter companies recommend to those thinking about weighing anchor and shipping out with their pet:

Pets are generally welcome on a case-by-case basis, but expect to pay damage deposits and cleaning fees. The dog needs to be seaworthy—he must be familiar with being on a boat, not bark incessantly, and not chew or sleep on the furnishings. You must properly dispose of pet feces, and your pet must be properly restrained when on the boat to ensure she does not fall overboard, run onto shore and get lost, or disturb others on board or in the anchorage or harbor.

Lastly, your pet must be healthy and free from infectious or contagious diseases. Charter companies also recommend that pets have the necessary documented vaccinations and health records. When traveling into some international areas, many companies suggest you bring a pet passport to facilitate interaction with governments that have strict pet health restrictions or quarantines.

If you are interested in exploring the seas with your dog, see the resources section for charter company contact information here and abroad.

Pets and the City

Some of my favorite United States cities are also favorites among pets, including Sherpa. **New York City** has many pet-friendly hotels, parks, restaurants, shops, and fun excursions guaranteed to delight the most discriminating pets and owners alike. Central Park is a great locale that will win both human and canine hearts. Acres and acres of open grassy areas are available to explore, and there are rocks to climb and small grottos and bridges that will transport you from the city's buzz. You'll also find a zoo and the carousel, free plays and concerts, and an abundance of food vendors to satisfy everyone's culinary cravings.

Best of all, visit New York's only doggie playground, "Canine Court," located downtown on the south side of Washington Square Park, at West 52nd and Broadway. This 14,000-square-foot area combines open land and obstacle courses.

The Hamptons are charming beach towns located only two to three hours from New York City, depending on traffic. These picturesque towns offer chic shops, great restaurants, and miles of pristine ocean where you and your pet can spend glorious days in the sun. Get there by hopping a ride on the Hampton Jitney (800-936-0440 or www.hamptonjitney.com). The Jitney allows dogs in carriers small enough to fit under your seat or on your lap. There is a $10 charge for pets.

San Francisco is another vacation destination that I highly recommend for pet lovers. This is an absolutely pet-fabulous city where you and your best friend can enjoy the city and all its activities together. I clearly remember how Sherpa enjoyed riding the cable cars. SuNae also loves them, but being a gal who likes to feel the wind in her hair, the ferries that rumble across the bay top her list of favorite activities.

San Francisco is truly a doggy paradise—a canine nirvana where many outdoor restaurants and distinctive shops cater to pooches, treating them as valued patrons. The city also offers off-leash doggie parks with hilly trails and beaches where doggies can run or sun. San Francisco also sports some of the greatest swimming spots that you and your pooch can enjoy together, including Carmel City Beach, Crissy Field,

Dillon Beach Resort, Esplanade Beach, Fort Funston, Garland Ranch Regional Park, Ocean Beach, Pet Camp's Dog Pool, and Point Isabel Regional Shoreline Park.

Boston is a gorgeous, culturally rich city that provides a great vacation destination for pets and owners alike. But owners please take note: All Boston parks have leash laws. The Emerald Necklace is the name given to the lush green series of beautifully maintained parks that extend from downtown Boston to Jamaica Plain. It's a lovely chain of greenery that flourishes amid man-made structures. Many of the parks can be reached by mass transportation, and pets are permitted on subways. If your pet can fit in a lap carrier, you can bring her on the subway at any time. Otherwise, your furry friend must be leashed and can ride only during off-peak hours and on weekends. Furry, feathered, or finned, all pets ride for free!

Nestled along the Charles River and reaching from the Museum of Science to Massachusetts Avenue, the Esplanade extends through most of old-town Boston. There is no more scenic spot in the city where you can jog, bicycle, skate, swim, or just stroll. The region between the Fiedler Bridge and the Hereford Street Bridge is a particularly great area for exercising your pooch. And if you want to take in a movie, the Hatch Shell amphitheater on the Esplanade becomes an outdoor movie theater on Friday nights in the summer. Movies are suitable for the entire family — and furry family members are always welcomed.

Café Esplanade, located alongside the Hatch Shell, offers

a wide variety of soups, sandwiches, and interesting beverages, all of which can be enjoyed on a great outdoor patio. At the back of the café is a dog bowl filled with fresh water for four-legged guests. If Fido or Daisy gets a yen for something sweet, find your way to Fi-Dough, a great doggie bakery featuring dog-gone good desserts and treats that will satisfy any sweet tooth!

For me, a day at the beach while vacationing in Boston means a trip to **Cape Cod.** The good news is that more and more hotels on the Cape are welcoming pets. The bad news is that most beaches do not allow dogs from May 15 to September 15. I love Truro, a popular stretch on the Atlantic Ocean where the sand is soft and the dunes are tall. Dogs are permitted only on leashes, but will enjoy running along the surf with you.

Key West is a great pet-friendly, relaxing destination. In this tropical paradise, such pets as domesticated parrots, iguanas, snakes, and cats accompany their owners on walks along the historic residential streets. I recommend that you head straight into Old Town. The historic district provides a taste of old Key West: architecture that blends the best of the Caribbean and New England—with plenty of clapboard, steep tin roofs, and welcoming porches. You might want to try bicycling or walking through Old Town. Duval Street is Key West's "main drag," where canines are found in abundance, usually sleeping at their owners' feet at the many sidewalk cafés. There are walking tours to the area's most famous attractions, including the cat-loving Hemingway's house, where pets are welcomed.

Troubleshooting

Sunburn is a great concern of mine while hiking, but especially at the beach or in a boat where sunlight is reflected off the sand and water. Your pet iguana may love the sun, but dogs of any breed can get their noses and ears sunburned; white dogs such as Westies, whose tender skin is not fully covered by fur, really sizzle in the sun. Humans need to share the sunscreen (at least SPF 15) with their dogs, putting it on their noses, ears, and fine white fur or exposed skin. Just make sure to keep it out of sensitive eyes and breathing passageways. I also advise that you bring your pet's carrier so that she has a place to escape from the sun; try a parasol, full-sized human beach umbrella, or boat canopy to provide the shade both you and your pet will need.

And in the evenings, you can wander over to the famous Sunset Festival on Mallory Square. This nightly event is a three-ring circus with jugglers, magicians, musicians, contortionists, and a couple of great pet-oriented shows.

If you'd like to swim with your four-legged friend, head over to Dog Beach at Louie's Backyard Restaurant. This is primarily a local swimming site with one of the best sandy bottoms in Key West. The beach is tiny, and lots of people take their dogs there. It is located between Louie's Backyard restaurant and the Reach Hotel over on the Atlantic Ocean side of town. There are also two dog beaches at the White Street Pier.

Troubleshooting

Always scoop your pet's poop. Carry poop bags (or appropriately sized plastic zipper bags) with you, and also in your car, and clean up after your pet wherever you go. If we are careless about our pet's habits, cities, parks, and businesses will begin revoking pet privileges.

Telluride, Colorado, is one of my favorite places for R, R & R—rest, "ruffs," and relaxation). In the 1960s, hippies and idealists trekked to this enchanting mountain enclave, hoping to retreat into a simple life, but its beauty was soon discovered. By the 1970s, this sleepy remote town had begun its transformation into a posh resort community. The historic section of the city is positively wonder-filled. Strict building codes have maintained a unique combination of both old Western and Victorian charm. Main Street is a unique mix of chic boutiques, outdoor recreation stores, and diverse restaurants that set up shop in the antique buildings.

Everyone here seems to have a dog, and they can be found lounging in front of bakeries, curled up in bars, and tagging along behind every bicycle rider, hiker, and runner. Dogs even have designated cars on the free gondola that spirits them over the hill to the Mountain Village resort. Dogs are allowed on the trails (250 of them) and in the backcountry. One of our favorite places to visit while we are there is Baked in Telluride, where patrons and their canines congregate on the front porch to enjoy a hearty and healthy meal.

chapter 8

if
gets lost
or

your pet

sick

First, pack this book because it is filled with useful advice should your pet become lost, injured, or sick while you are traveling. Second, if something does happen to your pet, stay calm and think clearly. Third, and most important, never give up. Nearly every week, it seems, we hear news stories about pets that have been reunited with their families months and years after being lost. If your pet gets sick or injured on the road, be prepared with a first-aid kit and the Web sites that list emergency vets. This chapter covers all these potential disasters and more, so reach for a highlighter and read on.

no pet left behind if your pet . . .

Loss Prevention

Pets live blessedly in the present, and their unbridled excitement over what is happening here and now is part of what endears them to us. The flip side of all this enthusiasm is that they don't stop to weigh the pros and cons of a potentially dangerous situation before chasing a squirrel into the street or dashing out a motel room door. So for safety's sake, it's up to us, as caring "parents," to keep a sharp eye on our inquisitive charges at all times.

It is never a good idea to leave your pet unattended, whether tethered to a parking meter outside a store or alone in a car because unattended pets are often stolen. If you absolutely must stop at a store or restaurant that doesn't permit pets, park in the shade, crack the windows, and keep watch over them from the store windows. If you can't order carry-out food, ask for a table near a window and door where you can tend to your car and your pet.

If you take your pet on a boat ride, she should be kept in a carrier that is fastened to a stationary support or she should wear a harness tethered a safe distance from the edge of the deck to ensure that she does not fall overboard or run onto the dock and get lost. Always use a pet flotation vest; these life savers have a handle so that if your pet does fall overboard, you can easily pull her back into the boat.

It bears repeating that pets should always wear collars and ID tags (fastening tags to a halter is more secure), but a microchip ID is the preferred form of identification. And remember to always carry a recent photo of your pet in your purse or billfold to help describe her if needed.

Train Your Pet Not to Get Lost

Leashes break, pets dash off when carriers are unzipped, or hotel and car doors are opened. What's an owner to do? If you have a small pet such as a rodent or bird, keep him in his travel cage and do not open the cage door unless the car or hotel room door is secured. Pack a net so that you can capture him if he does escape. If your pet is a chewer, make sure his cage is not plastic, but has chew-proof metal bars and metal floor.

A small hand towel makes an excellent substitute for a net if your bird, rodent, or cold-blooded pet escapes her cage. These pets don't recognize a towel as a threat, and you can easily toss it over them. The light weight of the towel will hold your pet still until you can reach under the towel and carefully pick the little critter up and return her to her cage.

A well-trained dog will automatically sit whenever she is heeling and her owner stops walking. The beauty of this "automatic sit" is that your pet won't tug on the leash or dash into traffic when you stop at a street intersection. Teaching these basics will help keep your pet safe—and welcomed—wherever you go. For more information on basic commands and obedience, see page 40.

Finding a Lost Pet

Despite our best efforts, sometimes pets become confused or frightened and dart out of car or hotel doors; carrier or cage doors fail; or leashes break or slip from our hands. If the worst happens, and your pet is lost en route or at your destination, contact the local police, animal control, local animal shelters, and veterinarians. Offer a detailed description and a recent photograph. Provide contact telephone numbers, preferably your cell phone number, and the numbers for your hotel, as well as nearby friends and family. Stay in constant communication until your pet is found.

You can also post photos and contact information on bulletin boards at your hotel, local pet shops, and veterinarian offices. And you can place ads in local papers featuring your pet's picture, as well as information on how to contact you. But don't forget to offer a reward—just don't say how much and don't pay it until your pet is returned.

Traverse your neighborhood, knock on doors, and hand out flyers. Look for your

no pet left behind if your pet . . .

pet outdoors in the afternoon and evening when there is less traffic noise, so that your pet will have a better chance of hearing you call his name or whistle. Drive slowly around the neighborhood because a pet often knows the sound of his owner's car and may appear.

If your pet is lost in air transit, contact the airline representative immediately and have the animal traced via the airline's automated baggage tracking system if your pet was checked baggage or through the cargo tracing system if your pet flew as air cargo or air freight. (**Remember:** make sure to label her travel crate with your flight information, cell phone number, and all other information that will help reunite you with your pet if he becomes lost.) Be sure that you have ID tags on your pet's collar, harness, and carrier. In case your pet loses her collar, microchip identification will allow her to be identified by any veterinarian's office or animal shelter. For more information on microchip IDs, see page 201.

Troubleshooting

When trying to find your pet, follow your instincts—if you know that your pet is a real trash hound, start your search by checking out the dumpsters at your hotel and nearby restaurants.

Lost Pet Flyers

Because speed is of the essence when you lose your pet, it's a good idea to create and print (either from your home computer or at a copy center) several "lost pet" posters before you leave for your trip. It's faster to run off more copies of a prepared poster than to take precious time creating one.

Your poster should include photographs, a list of emergency phone numbers for you including your cell number, contact information for your hotel, a local veterinary clinic, and nearby friends or relatives. It should also include a description of your pet, but deliberately leave off one or two distinguishing features, such as unique color pattern, unusual eye coloration, or scars. This will allow you to question callers carefully to make sure that they are legitimate and have actually

no pet left behind if your pet . . .

found your pet. Be sure to include the location where your pet was lost. You may also want to leave the pet's name off the poster, because it could be used by thieves to lure your pet.

Other Places to Look

If your pet is lost, visit the local department of animal control to see whether yours has been picked up. Look at all of the impounded animals, and if yours is not there, leave a description of your pet, a photo, and your contact information with the person at the front desk.

Also check the area's veterinary hospitals, the police department, and the humane society. Call the classified department of the local newspapers and ask them to scan the "found pet" notices in the edition that has not yet gone to press.

Give posters to the postman, local "beat" policeman, newspaper delivery person, UPS and FedEx drivers, and meter readers—any service people who travel a local route. These people travel continuously through the neighborhood and often are the first to spot stray animals.

New on the scene are online lost-and-found services such as Awolpet.com and PetFinder.com, where users can register the identification information for their pets in case they become lost or if they are lost, or even if they've found a stray. The service is open to individuals and also to veterinarians and shelters.

Troubleshooting

Don't just call lost-pet services; fax your lost-pet poster to their offices. This will give them a visible record of your pet's identification information, a photo, and your contact information.

Pet Insurance Programs

Interestingly, pet insurance is more common in Europe and Canada than in the United States, where it was introduced fairly recently. The oldest continuously operating United States pet insurance company was founded in 1980.

no pet left behind if your pet . . .

In order to make an educated decision about buying pet insurance, you need to ask a lot of questions, just as if you were considering insurance for yourself or your family.

Here are some of the most important questions to ask:

- How long has the company been in business?
- Is your veterinarian familiar with the company?
- Does the company work like an HMO, or can you go to any licensed veterinarian in the world, without preauthorization?
- Does the policy offer wellness coverage—reimbursements for preventive measures such as exams, vaccinations, heartworm protection, and neutering?
- Are there "pre-existing condition" drawbacks?
- Are there common ailments, such as hip dysphasia, that are not covered?
- How does the cost compare to costs by other providers?

Many insurers also provide traveler-friendly coverage, such as boarding fees, theft or loss, advertising, or reward, liability, and accidental damage. Some even offer pet travel insurance; ask and compare the costs and benefits to find the right fit. The American Society for the Prevention of Cruelty to Animals (ASPCA) also provides an insurance program. For more information, see resources, page 203.

reso

urces

Airlines That Accept Pets in Cabin

This alphabetical list of airlines shows you which ones permit small pets (under 20 pounds) to travel in the cabin with you—in an authorized carrier under the seat. Keep in mind that airline policies and under-the-seat dimensions do change, so be sure to check with the airline early in your planning process.

Name	Phone/Web site	Pets in Cabin	Types of Pet Allowed
Aer Arann	353-818-2102 www.aerarann.com	No	
Aer Lingus	800-474-7424 www.aerlingus.com	No	
Aero Litoral, SA de CV	800-369-8540 www.aerolitoral.com	No	
Aero Mexico	800-237-6639 www.aeromexico.com	No	
Aeroflot Russian Airlines	888-340-6400 www.aeroflot.ru/eng/	Yes	cats, dogs, birds
Aerolineas Argentina	800-333-0276 www.aerolineas.com.ar/	No	
Air Berlin	49 (0)1805-737 800 www.airberlin.com	Yes	cats, dogs
Air Canada	888-247-2262 www.aircanada.com	No	
Air Europa	902-401-501 www.air-europa.com	Yes	cats, dogs, birds, hamsters

Name	Phone/Web site	Pets in Cabin	Types of Pet Allowed
Air France	800-525-3663 www.airfrance.com	Yes	cats, dogs Note: First segment must be via Paris. Pets are not permitted in cabin on flights to the UK.
Air India	800-223-7776 www.airindia.com	Yes	
Air Jamaica	800-523-5585 www.airjamaica.com	No	
Air Midwest, Inc.	316-942-8137 www.midwestairlines.com	Yes	
Air Pacific	679-672-0777 www.airpacific.com	No	
Air Wisconsin Airlines Corp.	920-749-4188 www.airwis.com	Yes	
Air Wisconsin UA Express	800-864-8331	Yes	
AirTran Airways	800-247-7626 www.airtran.com	Yes	domesticated cats, dogs, birds
Alaska Airlines/Horizon Air	800-252-7522 www.alaskaair.com	Yes	dogs, cats, rabbits, household birds, tropical fish
Alitalia	800-223-5730 www.alitalia.com	Yes	

Name	Phone/Web site	Pets in Cabin	Types of Pet Allowed
All Nippon Airlines	800-235-9262 www.ana.co.jp/eng/	Yes	cats, dogs
Allegheny Airlines, Inc.	717-948-5400 www.usairways.com	Yes	
Allegiant Airlines	888-594-6937 www.allegiantair.com	Yes	cats, dogs
Aloha Airlines	800-367-5250 www.alohaairlines.com	Yes	
Aloha Islandair, Inc.	808-836-7693 www.islandair.com	No	
America West Airlines	800-235-9292 www.americawest.com	Yes	
American Airlines	800-433-7300 www.aa.com	Yes	cats, dogs Note: The kennel may contain two dogs or two cats, but they must be the same species, ages between eight weeks and six months and weigh less than twenty pounds. American Airlines no longer allows birds in cabin, nor does it allow any pets in cabin on flights more than six hours, which rules out any European travel.
American Eagle Airlines	817-963-1234 www.aa.com	Yes	

no pet left behind resources

Name	Phone/Web site	Pets in Cabin	Types of Pet Allowed
Asiana Airlines	800-227-4262 http://us.flyasiana.com	Yes	cats, dogs
Astral Aviation, Inc.	414-570-2300 www.astral-aviation.com	No	
TA (American Trans Air)	800-225-2995 www.ata.com	Yes	cats, dogs, small birds Note: Two puppies or two kittens, eight weeks to six months of age, weighing less than twenty pounds (nine kilograms) each may be transported in the same travel container.
Atlantic Coast Airlines, Inc.	703-650-6000	Yes	
Atlantic Southeast Airlines	404-766-1400 www.flyasa.com	Yes	
Austrian Airlines	718-670-8600 www.aua.com	Yes	cats, dogs
Big Sky Transportation	406-247-3910 www.bigskyair.com	No	
British Airways	800-247-9297 www.britishairways.com	No	
British Midland Airways	800-788-0555 www.flybmi.com	No	
Cape Air	508-790-3122 www.flycapeair.com	Yes	

Name	Phone/Web site	Pets in Cabin	Types of Pet Allowed
Cathay Pacific	800-233-2742 www.cathaypacific.com	No	
Champion Air	888-883-7131 www.championair.com	No	
Chautauqua Airlines, Inc.	317-484-6000 www.flychautauqua.com	Yes	
Chicago Express Airlines	773-948-8017 www.ata.com	Yes	
China Airlines	800-227-5118 www.china-airlines.com	Yes	
Colgan Air, Inc.	703-368-8880 www.colganair.com	Yes	
Comair Inc.	859-767-2550 www.comair.com	Yes	
CommutAir	518-562-2700 www.commutair.com	Yes	
Continental Airlines	800-525-9280 www.continental.com	Yes	cats, dogs, pet rabbits, household birds
Delta Airlines	800-221-1212 www.delta.com	Yes	cats, dogs, birds, ferrets, rabbits, hamsters, guinea pigs Note: Monkeys, pot-bellied pigs, reptiles, frogs, mice, rats, sugar gliders, and spiders are not permitted.

Name	Phone/Web site	Pets in Cabin	Types of Pet Allowed
Eagle Canyon Airlines, Inc.	702-638-3215 www.scenic.com	Yes	
El Al Israeli Airlines	800-223-6700 www.elal.com/ELAL/English /States/General	Yes	cats, dogs, household birds
EVA Airways Corporation	800-695-1188 www.evaair.com	Yes	
Executive Airlines, Inc.	787-253-6403 www.executive-airlines.com	Yes	
ExpressJet Holdings, Inc.	713-324-2639 www.expressjet.com	Yes	
Finnair Oyj	800-950-5000 www.finnair.com	Yes	small dogs, cats, guinea pigs, hamsters, rabbits Note: Other pets, such as birds, snakes, lizards and insects, are not permitted in cabin.
Frontier Airlines	800-432-1359 www.frontierairlines.com	No	
Great Lakes Aviation, Ltd.	307-432-7000 www.greatlakesav.com	Yes	
Gulfstream International	954-266-3000 www.gulfstreamair.com	Yes	

Name	Phone/Web site	Pets in Cabin	Types of Pet Allowed
Hawaiian Airlines	800-367-5320 www.hawaiianair.com	Yes	cats, dogs (with breed restrictions) Note: Animals are permitted in cabin only on inter-island flights and flights leaving the State of Hawaii.
Horizon Air	206-241-6757 www.alaskaair.com	Yes	
Iberia - Lineas Aereas	800-772-4642	Yes	cats, dogs, small birds Note: The carrier may be shared, provided the animals inside are used to cohabitation and that the total weight of animals and carrier does not exceed ten pounds (eight kilograms).
Icelandair	800-223-5500 www.icelandair.com	No	
Japan Airlines International	800-525-3663 www.jal.com	No	
Jet Blue	800-JETBLUE (800-538-2583) www.jetblue.com	Yes	cats, dogs
KLM Royal Dutch Airlines	800 -374-7747 www.klm.com	Yes	one adult cat or dog, or no more than two puppies or kittens younger than six

Name	Phone/Web site	Pets in Cabin	Types of Pet Allowed
			months, of comparable size, and under twenty pounds. Note: Dogs and cats cannot travel in the same carrier. Also, no pets in cabin to Hawaii, the United Kingdom, and Hong Kong.
Korean Air	800-438-5000 www.koreanair.com	Yes	cats, dogs, birds
L'Avion Airlines	866-692-6759 www.lavion.com	Yes	cats, dogs
Lan Chile Airlines Lan Equador Airlines Lan Peru Airlines	800-735-2445 www.lan.com	No	
LOT Polish Airlines	800-223-0593 www.lot.com	Yes	cats, dogs
Lufthansa Airlines	800-645-3880 www.lufthansa.com	Yes	cats, dogs
Malaysia Airlines	800-552-9264 www.malaysiaairlines.com	No	
Maxjet Airways	800-435-9629 www.maxjet.com	No	
Mesa Airlines, Inc.	602-685-4000 www.mesa-air.com	Yes	

Name	Phone/Web site	Pets in Cabin	Types of Pet Allowed
Mesaba Aviation, Inc.	612-713-6320 www.mesaba.com	Yes	
Mexicana Airlines	800-531-7921 www.mexicana.com	Yes	cats, dogs
Midwest Airlines	800-452-2022 www.midwestairlines.com	Yes	small dogs
Northwest Airlines	800-225-2525 www.nwa.com	Yes	small dogs, cats, household birds Note: Birds are allowed in every state but Hawaii. Note: Two small pets of the same species may share a carrier if they are between three and six months, are compatible, and weigh under fifteen pounds (including the carrier), or if they are an adult mother and off-spring under four months.
Olympic Airways	800-223-1226 www.olympicairlines.com	Yes	cats, dogs
Pacific Wings, Inc.	808-873-0877 www.pacificwings.com	Yes	
Philippine Airlines	800-435-9725 www.philippineairlines.com	No	
Qantas Airways	800-227-4500 www.qantas.com.au	No	

Name	Phone/Web site	Pets in Cabin	Types of Pet Allowed
Royal Air Maroc	www.royalairmaroc.com	Yes	cats, dogs, birds
SAS Scandinavian	800-221-2350 www.flysas.com	Yes	cats, dogs
Scot Airways	0870-6060707 www.scotairways.co.uk	Yes	
Singapore Airlines	800-742-3333 www.singaporeair.com	No	
Song Airlines	800-359-7664 www.delta.com	Yes	
South African Airways	800-722-9675 www.flysaa.com	No	
Southwest Airlines	800-435-9792 www.southwest.com	No	
Spirit Airlines	800-772-7117 www.spiritair.com	Yes	cat, dogs, domestic birds
Sun Country Airlines	800-359-6786 www.suncountry.com	Yes	
SWISS International Airlines	877-359-7947 www.swiss.com	Yes	cats, dogs, songbirds
TACA International Airlines	800-535-8782 www.taca.com	Yes	cats, dogs

Name	Phone/Web site	Pets in Cabin	Types of Pet Allowed
TAP–Air Portugal	800-221-7370 www.flytap.com	Yes	cats, dogs
Ted Airlines	800-864-8331 www.flyted.com	Yes	cats, dogs, small birds
Thai Airways	800-426-5204 www.thaiair.com	Yes	cats, dogs
Tunis Air	002-1671-941-285 www.tunisair.com	Yes	
Turkish Air	800-872-3000 www.thy.com	Yes	fully weaned dogs or cats, domesticated household birds (canaries, finches, parakeets) Note: Tropical birds such as parrots are not allowed.
United Airlines	800-241-6522 www.ual.com	Yes	
US Airways	800-428-4322 www.usair.com	Yes	one small domestic dog, cat, bird, or small aquarium fish (less than four inches) Note: Only dogs and cats are allowed to or from Mexico and Costa Rica.
USA3000 Airlines	800-872-3000 www.usa3000.com	Yes	cats, dogs

no pet left behind resources

Name	Phone/Web site	Pets in Cabin	Types of Pet Allowed
Varig SA Airlines	800-468-2744 www.varig.com	Yes	dogs
Virgin Atlantic Airways Ltd.	800-862-8621 www.virgin-atlantic.com	No	
West Jet	800-538-5696 www.westjet.com	Yes	cats, dogs, rabbits, birds

General Travel Information

www.petsonthego.com

The definitive guide for information on pet-friendly accommodations, restaurants, shops, tours, and recreational resources, this site also lists the rules for domestic and international pet travel.

www.pettravel.com

This is the place to go when you want info about where you and your pet can stay, what to see and do in the area, and which items you need to take that will make your life and your pet's life just a bit easier.

www.takeyourpet.com

Information on discounts at thousands of pet-friendly bed-and-breakfasts, hotels, motels, inns, and resorts can be found at this site, which also offers a directory of more than 20,000 pet-friendly lodgings throughout the United States. You'll also find listed here thousands of animal hospitals, shelters, groomers, kennels and boarding facilities, exercise and sitting services, pet food and supply stores, and veterinarians.

Big Cities

www.urbanhound.com

Here you'll find everything you need to know about traveling with your dog in Chicago, New York, and San Francisco.

www.petfriendlytravel.com

This site offers lots of information on beaches, parks, and other recreational interests for you and your pet.

State Parks, National Parks, and Dog Camps

www.hikewithyourdog.com

This great resource helps you find tail-friendly trails in national parks and forests throughout the United States.

Top 5 National Parks

(Ratings are based on sights to see and places to walk or hike with dogs.)

1. Grand Canyon, AZ
2. Acadia, ME
3. Shenandoah, VA
4. Yosemite, CA
5. North Cascades, WA

Dog Camps

Dog camps are often an excellent way to explore new dog activities, but they can vary widely. Some are intended as vacations with your dog. Others cater to people who are already competing in a dog sport and want to improve their skills.

Camp Dog Wood North

Lake Joseph, Ontario, Canada

www.campdogwoodnorth.com

This camp offers an introduction to a variety of dog sports and dog training methods, obedience, rally, freestyle, fly ball, agility, and more.

Barking Hills Country Club
Hackettstown, NJ
www.barkinghills.com
Activities include obedience, lure coursing, agility, fly ball, and carting. The camp is also active in pet-assisted therapy programs.

Camp Barking Hills
Lebanon, NJ
www.campbarkinghills.com
This weekend camp is for dogs and owners who want to learn new things and explore a variety of new activities in a relaxing atmosphere.

Dog Days of Wisconsin Summer Camp
Stevens Point, WI
www.dogcamp.com
Participate in one of the scheduled activities or just watch the sunset on a hill with crickets chirping around you at this camp, 140 miles northwest of Milwaukee.

Camp Gone to the Dogs
VT (Various locations)
www.camp-gone-to-the-dogs.com
Perhaps the most well known of the dog camps, this camp offers a week-long session with introductions to fly ball, herding, agility, clicker training, canine nutrition, and more.

no pet left behind resources

Camp Winnaribbun

Lake Tahoe, NV

www.campw.com

Participate in obedience, agility, herding, tracking, nature talks, massage therapy, wonderful campfires, storytelling, and more.

Camp Unleashed

The Berkshires, MA

www.campunleashed.com

This camps offers agility courses, canine water sports, freestyle, canine massage, clicker training, Tellington Touch, and much more.

Dog Daze at the Highlands

Fort Washington, PA

This three-day camp in July provides an introduction to various dog activities.

Dog Scout Camp

Nationwide

www.dogscouts.com

Unlike other dog camps that are primarily about recreation, Dog Scout Camp tries to teach your dog skills that will serve her in real life and teaches owners how to better communicate with their dogs.

Pet-Friendly Boat Charters

Blue Pacific Yacht Charters
1519 Foreshore Walk
Granville Island, Vancouver
British Columbia, Canada V6H 3X3
800-237-2392, 604-682-2161
Note: If the boat requires any additional cleanup because of the pet, an additional $45 cleaning charge will apply.

BVI Yacht Charters
P.O. Box 11156
St. Thomas, US Virgin Islands 00801
Phone: 284-494-4289, Fax: 284-494-6552
Note: The Virgin Island veterinary division must be given at least a twenty-four-hour notice of your confirmed arrival date. Call the Agriculture Department at 284-495-2532.

Cruising in Paradise
31 Empress Pines Drive
Nesconset, NY 11767
Phone: 800-874-2584, Fax: 631-471-7315

GPSC Charters Ltd.
600 St. Andrews Rd.
Philadelphia, PA 19118
800-732-6786

no pet left behind resources

Hinckley Crewed Charters

15 Mansell Lane, P.O. Box Six
Southwest Harbor, ME 04679
Phone: 800-504-2305, 207-244-0122, Fax: 207-244-0156
Note: Whether pets are accepted is entirely up to the owner and crew.

Nanaimo Charters

1690 Stewart Ave.
Nanaimo, BC, Canada, V9S 4E1
Note: In some circumstances an additional cleanup fee is charged to cover the extra cleaning.

North Huron Charters

1266 Queen St. E.
Sault Ste Marie, ON, Canada, P6A 2E8
Phone: 705-253-9346, Fax: 705-253-9346
Note:: North Huron generally prefers small pets who have been boating before.

Sacks Yachts

1600 SE 17th Street, Suite 418
Fort Lauderdale, FL 33316
Phone: 954-764-7742, Fax: 954-523-3769
Note: A damage deposit is generally requested.

Small Ship Cruises

545 - 35th Ave. NE
St. Petersburg, FL 33704
800-290-0077
www.smallshipcruises.com

Lodgings
General Information

Pet-friendly Timeshares and Condos
www.staynplay.net/pet-friendly.htm

Doris Day's Pet-friendly Hotel
The Cypress Inn, Carmel-by-the-Sea, CA
www.cypress-inn.com

PetsMart Hotel and Day Camp
www.petshotel.petsmart.com
This is a wonderful place for your pet to visit while you take a day trip. Grooming, veterinary, and activity services are all included.

Pet-friendly Places to Stay in Major Cities

Boston
Boston Harbor Hotel
Rowes Wharf
617-439-7000

The Colonnade Hotel
120 Huntington Avenue
617-424-7000

no pet left behind resources

Elliot Suite Hotel
370 Commonwealth Avenue
617-267-1607

The Fairmont Copley Plaza
138 St. James Avenue
617-267-5300

Four Seasons Hotel
Boylston Street
617-338-4400

Hilton Back Bay
40 Dalton Street
617-236-1100

Seaport Hotel
1 Seaport Lane
617-385-4000

Sheraton and the Prudential Center
39 Dalton Street
617-236-2000

The Westin at Copley Place
10 Washington Avenue
617-262-9600

Key West
Ambrosia House
622 Fleming Street
305-296-9838

Atlantic Shores Resort
510 South Street
888-324-2995

Avalon B&B
1317 Duval Street
900-848-1317

Chelsea House
707 Truman Avenue
800-845-8859

Courtney's Place
720 Whitemarsh Lane
800-869-4639

The Cuban Club
1108 Duval Street
305-294-5269

Curry Mansion Inn
511 Caroline Street
800-253-3466

Douglas House
419 Amelia Street
305-294-5269

Frances Street Bottle Inn
535 Frances Street
305-294-8530

Key Lodge Motel
1004 Duval Street
305-296-9915

Key West Hideaways
915 Eisenhower Drive
888-822-5840

Old Customs House Inn
124 Duval Street
305-294-8507

Sea Isle Resort
915 Windsor Lane
305-294-5188

Seascape Tropical Inn and Cottages
420 Olivia Street
800-765-6438

Speakeasy Inn
1117 Duval Street
800-217-4884

Southernmost Point Guest House
1327 Duval Street
305-294-0715

Sunrise Key West
3685 Seaside Drive
888-723-5200

Travelers Palm Garden Cottage
815 Catherine Street
800-294-9560

New York City
Affinia Dumont Hotel
150 East 34th Street
212-481-7600

Affinia Fifty
155 E. 50th Street
212-751-5710

Best Western President Hotel
234 W. 48th Street
212-632-9000

no pet left behind resources

The Carlyle
35 East 76th Street
212-744-1600

Crowne Plaza Manhattan
1605 Broadway
212-986-1758

Four Seasons
57 East 57th Street
212-758-5700

Holiday Inn Wall Street
15 Gold Street
212-232-7700

Howard Johnson Plaza Hotel
851 Eighth Avenue
212-581-4100

Hotel Plaza Athenee
37 East 64th Street
212-734-9100

The Mansfield Hotel
12 West 44th Street
212-277-8700

Marriott Marquis
1535 Broadway Street
866-671-4302

The Meridian
18 W. 57th Street
212-397-5170

New York Palace
455 Madison Avenue
212-888-0131

New York's Hotel Pennsylvania
401 Seventh Avenue
800-671-9207

On The Ave Hotel
2178 Broadway (77th Street)
212-362-1100

The Pierre
2 East 61st Street
212-838-8000

The Ritz Carlton Hotel
50 Central Park South
212-308-9100

Royalton Hotel
44 W. 44th Street
212-869-4400

Sheraton Manhattan
790 Seventh Avenue
212-581-3300

Sheraton New York Hotel
811 Seventh Avenue
800-671-9207

Soho Grand Hotel
310 W. Broadway Street
212-965-3000

TriBeCa Grand Hotel
Two Avenue of the Americas
212-519-6600

Waldorf Towers
100 E. 50th Street
212-355-3100

W New York - The Court
130 East 39th Street
212-685-1100

W New York - The Tuscany
120 East 39th Street
212-686-1600

W New York - Union Square
201 Park Avenue South
212-253-9119

Westin Essex House
160 Central Park S.
212-247-0300

Westin New York at Times Square
270 W. 43rd Street
212-201-2700

San Francisco
Beresford Arms
701 Post Street
415-673-2600

Beresford Hotel
635 Sutter Street
415-673-9900
Best Western Civic Center
364 Ninth Street
415-621-2826

Campton Place
340 Stockton Street
415-955-5526

Days Inn
2358 Lombard Street
415-922-2010

Edwardian Hotel
1668 Market Street
415-864-1271

Fairmont Hotel San Francisco
950 Mason Street
415-397-1468

Golden Gate Hotel
775 Bush Street
415-392-3702

Hayes Valley Inn
417 Gough Street
415-431-9131

Hotel Monaco
501 Geary Street
415-292-0100

Hotel Nikko
222 Mason Street
415-394-1111

Hotel Triton
342 Grant Avenue
415-394-0500

Laurel Inn
444 Presidio Avenue
415-567-8467

The Inn San Francisco
943 S. Van Ness Avenue
415-641-0188

Marriott
55 Fourth Street
415-957-9425

Marriott - Fisherman's Wharf
1250 Columbus Avenue
415-775-7555

Mandarin Oriental Hotel
222 Sansome Street
415-986-2020

Omni San Francisco
500 California South
415-677-9494

Pacific Heights Inn
1555 Union Street
415-776-3310

Pan Pacific Hotel
500 Post Street
415-771-8600

The Prescott Hotel
545 Post Street
415-563-0303

Serrano Hotel
405 Taylor Street
415-885-2500

Travelodge by the Bay
1450 Lombard Street
415-673-0691

Travelodge San Francisco Central
1707 Market Street
415-621-6775

Vagabond Inn
222 S. Airport Boulevard
650-589-9055

Washington Square Inn
1660 Stockton Street
415-981-4220

Telluride
The Cabins and Penthouses at the Peaks
109 Sunny Ridge
800-996-3426

Hotel Columbia
300 San Juan Avenue
800-201-9505

The Peaks Resort and Spa
136 Country Club Drive
866-282-4557

River Club
550 W. Depot Avenue
970-728-3986

Telluride Mountainside Inn
333 S. Davis Street
970-728-1950

The Hotel Telluride
199 N. Comet Street
970-369-1188

International Travel

The Electronic Embassy at *www.embassy.org* provides information on each of the embassies in Washington, DC, with links to Web-based resources where available.

Note: The address and telephone numbers given here are for embassy headquarters in Washington, DC. You can find information on local Consulate Generals and their jurisdictions on the embassy's main Web site.

Embassy of the Argentina Republic
www.embassyofargentina-usa.org
1600 New Hampshire Avenue NW
Washington, DC 20009
202-238-6400
Fax: 202-332-3171

Embassy of Australia
1601 Massachusetts Avenue NW
Washington, DC 20036-2273
202-797-3000
Fax: 202-799-3168

Embassy of Austria
www.austria.org
3524 International Court, NW
Washington, DC 20008-3027

202-895-6700
Fax: 202-895-6750

Embassy of Belgium
www.diplobel.org/usa
3330 Garfield Street NW
Washington, DC 20008
202-333-6900
Fax: 202-338-4960

British Embassy for Britain, Northern Ireland, Scotland, and Wales
www.britainusa.com
3100 Massachusetts Avenue NW
Washington, DC 20008
202-588-7800

Embassy of Brazil
www.consulatebrazil.org
3009 Whitehaven Street
Washington, DC 20008
202-238-2818

Embassy of Canada
www.canadianembassy.org
501 Pennsylvania Avenue NW
Washington, DC 20001-2114
202-682-1740
Fax: 202-682-7619

**Embassy of the People's
Republic of China**
2300 Connecticut Avenue NW
Washington, DC 20008
202-338-6688
Fax: 202-588-9760

Embassy of Colombia
www.colombiaemb.org
1101 17th Street NW, Suite 1007
Washington, DC 20036
202-332-7476
Fax: 202-332-7180

Embassy of Costa Rica
www.costarica-embassy.org
2112 S Street NW
Washington, DC 20008
202-328-6628
Fax: 202-234-6950

Embassy of Cyprus
www.kypros.org/Embassy
2211 R Street NW
Washington, DC 20008
202-462-5772
Fax: 202-483-6710

Embassy of the Czech Republic
3900 Spring of Freedom Street NW
Washington, DC 20008
202-274-9100
Fax: 202-966-8540

**Embassy of Denmark
(The Royal Danish Embassy)**
www.ambwashington.um.dk/en
3200 Whitehaven Street NW
Washington, DC 20008
202-234-4300
Fax: 202-328-1470

Embassy of the Arab Republic of Egypt
www.egyptembassy.us
3521 International Court NW
Washington, DC 20008
202-895-5400
Fax: 202-244-4319

Embassy of Finland
www.finland.org
3301 Massachusetts Avenue NW
Washington, DC 20008
202-298-5800
Fax: 202-298-6030

Embassy of France
www.consulfrance-washington.org
5101 Reservoir Road NW
Washington, DC 20007-2185
202-944-6195
Fax: 202-944-6148

**Embassy of the Federal
Republic of Germany**
www.germany-info.org
4645 Reservoir Road NW
Washington, DC 20007-1998
202-298-8140
Fax: 202-298-4249

Embassy of Greece
www.greekembassy.org
2211 Massachusetts Avenue NW
Washington, DC 20008
202-939-1306
Fax: 202-234-2803

Embassy of The Holy See (Vatican)
Apostolic Nunciature, The Holy See
3339 Massachusetts Avenue NW
Washington, DC 20008
202-333-7121

Embassy of Hungary
www.huembwas.org
3910 Shoemaker Street NW
Washington, DC 20008
202-362-6730
Fax: 202-966-8135

Embassy of India
www.indianembassy.org
2536 Massachusetts Avenue NW
Washington, DC 20008
202-939-9806
Fax: 202-797-4693

Embassy of Ireland
http://irelandemb.org
2234 Massachusetts Avenue NW
Washington, DC 20008
202-462-3939
Fax: 202-232-5993

Embassy of Israel
www.israelemb.org
3514 International Drive NW
Washington, DC 20008
202-364-5527

Embassy of Italy
www.italyemb.org
3000 Whitehaven Street NW
Washington, DC 20008
202-612-4405
Fax: 202-518-2142

Embassy of Japan
www.us.emb-japan.go.jp/
english/html/index.htm
2520 Massachusetts Avenue NW
Washington, DC 20008
202-238-6700

Embassy of Kenya
www.kenyaembassy.com
2249 R Street NW
Washington, DC 20008
202-37-6101
Fax: 202-462-3829

Embassy of Korea
www.koreaembassy.org
2320 Massachusetts Avenue NW
Washington, DC 20008
202-939-5654
Fax: 202-342-1597

**Embassy of the Grand
Duchy of Luxembourg**
www.luxembourg-usa.org
2200 Massachusetts Avenue
Washington, DC 20008
202-265-4171
Fax: 202-328-8270

Embassy of Mexico
www.mexonline.com/consulate.htm
1911 Pennsylvania NW
Washington, DC 20006
202-736-1000
Fax: 202-234-4498

Embassy of Morocco
www.africa.upenn.edu/Country_Specific/
Morocco_emb.html
1601 21st Street NW
Washington, DC 20009
202-462-7979 to 7982
Fax: 202-265-0161

Embassy of The Royal Netherlands
www.netherlands-embassy.org
4200 Linnean Avenue NW
Washington, DC 20008
202-244-5300
Fax: 202-362-3440

Embassy of New Zealand
www.nzembassy.com
37 Observatory Circle NW
Washington, DC 20008
202-328-4800
Fax: 202-667-5227

The Royal Embassy of Norway
www.invanor.no/usa
2720 34th Street NW
Washington, DC 20008
202-944-8996
Fax: 202-337-0870

Embassy of Oman
2535 Belmont Road NW
Washington, DC 20008
202-387-1980/1982
Fax: 202-745-4933

**Embassy of The Islamic
Republic of Pakistan**
www.embassyofpakistan.org
3517 International Court NW
Washington, DC 20008
202-243-6500

Embassy of The Republic of Panama
2862 McGill Terrace NW
Washington, DC 20008
202-483-1407

Embassy of Peru
www.peruvianembassy.us
1700 Massachusetts Avenue NW
Washington, DC 20036-1903
800-535-3953

**Embassy of the Republic
of the Philippines**
http://www.philippineembassy-usa.org/
1600 Massachusetts Avenue NW
Washington, DC 20036
202-467-9300
Fax: 202-467-9417

Embassy of the Republic of Poland
www.polandembassy.org
2224 Wyoming Avenue NW
Washington, DC 20008-3992
202-234-3800
Fax: 202-328-2152

Embassy of the Republic of Portugal
www.portugalemb.org
2125 Kalorama Road NW
Washington, DC 20008
202-328-8610
Fax: 202-462-3726

Embassy of the State of Qatar
www.qatarembassy.net/consular.asp
2555 M Street NW
Washington, DC 20037-1305
202-274-1603
Fax: 202-237-9880

Embassy of the Republic of Singapore
www.mfa.gov.sg/washington/
3501 International Place NW
Washington, DC 20008
202-537-3100
Fax: 202-537-7086

Embassy of South Africa
www.saembassy.org
3051 Massachusetts Avenue NW
Washington, DC 20008
202-232-4400
Fax: 202-265-1607

Embassy of Spain
www.spainemb.org
2375 Pennsylvania Avenue NW
Washington, DC 20037
202-728-2330
Fax: 202-728-2302

Embassy of Sweden
www.swedenabroad.com/washington
1501 M Street NW, Suite 900
Washington, DC 20005-1702
202-467-2600
Fax: 202-467-2699

Embassy of Switzerland
www.eda.admin.ch/washington
2900 Cathedral Avenue NW
Washington, DC 20008-3499
202-745-7900
Fax: 202-387-2564

Royal Thai Embassy
www.thaiembdc.org
1024 Wisconsin Avenue NW, Suite 101
Washington, DC 20007
202-298-4814
Fax: 202-944-3611

Embassy of the Republic of Turkey
www.turkishembassy.org
2525 Massachusetts Avenue, NW
Washington, DC 20008
202-612-6700
Fax: 202-612-6744

Embassy of Uruguay
http://www.uruwashi.org
1913 I Street NW
Washington, DC 20006
202-331-1313
Fax: 202-331-8142

Embassy of Venezuela
embajada@embavenez-us.org
1099 30th Street NW
Washington, DC 20007
202-342-2214
Fax: 202-342-6820

Agencies for Health Certificates and Import Requirements

United States
United States Department of Agriculture (USDA)
www.usda.gov

Animal and Plant Health Inspection Service (APHIS)
www.aphis.usda.gov

These sites provide general information about traveling with your pet, including domestic state regulations and USDA-APHIS veterinary services. You can also obtain import permits for birds and arrange for inspection by an APHIS-approved veterinarian in order to get the appropriate veterinary certificates for international travel.

USDA Animal Import Center
Quarantine facilities in the United States (most birds—with the exception of ones coming from Canada—must be quarantined for at least thirty days in one of these three facilities):

New York, NY   718-552-1727
Miami, FL   305-526-2926
Los Angeles, CA   310-725-1970

U.S. Centers for Disease Control and Prevention
www.cdc.gov

U.S. Customs Service
www.cbp.gov

The National Center for Import and Export
4700 River Road
Riverdale, MD 20737
301-734-8364
Fax: 301-734-4704

American Veterinary Medical Organization
www.avma.org/careforanimals/animatedjourneys/livingwithpets/stateregs.asp
This site offers everything you need to know about interstate travel regulations.

Canada
Canadian Food Inspection Agency (CFIA)
www.inspection.gc.ca
613-225-2342
Here you'll find information about pet importation into Canada.

Canadian Wildlife Service
www.cws-scf.ec.gc.ca/
613-997-1840
This service provides information on which animals need Convention on International Trade in Endangered Species (CITES) import permits, as well as application forms for permits. It also provides information about pet importation and exportation.

International
Blue Pet Passport
www.pet-passport.com
Every pet must have a Blue Pet Passport when traveling between EU Countries or the Form EU998 if entering the EU from another country.

Department for Environment, Food, and Rural Affairs

www.defra.gov.uk

Helpline: 44 (0)870 241 1710 (Monday to Friday - 8:30 a.m. to 5 p.m. UK time)

This department provides all information pertaining to the Pet Travel Scheme (PETS) and procedures, and has up-to-date import and export details.

PetTravel.com

www.pettravel.com/passportnew.cfm

This is a good site for all pet immigration, quarantine, and passport information, including the EU form 998 Veterinary Certificate, for travel to any countries of the European Union.

International Boat and Train Travel

International Sea Transport Companies accepting PETS

Brittany Ferries

www.brittany-ferries.co.uk

44 (0)8705 360360

Serves Great Britain, France, Spain

Condor Ferries

www.condorferries.co.uk

44 (0)1205 761551

Serves Guernsey, Jersey, St. Malo, Western France

DFDS Seaways

www.dfdsseaways.co.uk

44 (0)805 333111

Serves Great Britain, Norway, Denmark, Holland

Hoverspeed
www.hoverspeed.com
44 (0)870 2408070
Serves Dover to Calais

Norfolkline Shipping
www.norfolkline.com
44 (0)870 8701020
Channel crossings only

Sea France
www.seafrance.com
44 (0)805 711711
Serves Dover to Calais

Speedferries
www.speedferries.com
44(0)870 2200570
Serves Great Britain, France

Stena Line
www.stenaline.com
44 (0)1255 243333
Serves Belgium, Denmark, Germany,
Great Britain, Ireland, Netherlands,
Norway, Poland, Sweden

Superfast Ferries
www.superfast.com
44 (0)870 2340870
Serves all points in the North, Adriatic,
and Baltic Seas

Transmanche Ferries
www.aferry.to
44 (0)1273 612875
Serves France, Great Britain, Ireland,
Spain, Holland

Trains
Eurotunnel
www.eurotunnel.co.uk/english/en-pas-
senger/PETS.asp
44 (0)8705 353535

Eurail
www.eurail.com
800-274-8724

Japan Rail Pass
www.jreast.co.jp/e/index.html
Orient Express
www.luxury-trains.co.uk

Pet Recovery Information

The AKC Companion Animal Recovery

www.akccar.org

5580 Centerview Drive, Suite 250

Raleigh, NC 27606-3389

800-252-7894

The Avid Microchip

www.avidmicrochip.com

Note: Request the EuroChip version if you are traveling to Europe. This is the microchip version that is most widely read in Europe, as well as in some other countries. AVID also has a program called PetTrac, which is in place in the United States, England, and Mexico, and is rapidly being adopted in most of Europe.

HomeAgain Microchip

www.homeagain.com

Note: This microchip conforms to Annex A 2.1 of the ISO 11785, which is the new standard issued by the member countries of the European Union. It can be read by all scanners manufactured by Digital Angel distributed around the world.

Web sites for Locating Lost Pets

www.hsus.org/pets/ (the Humane Society)

www.petfinder.com

www.1-800-Save-A-Pet.com

www.Pets4you.com

www.awolpet.com

Veterinarian Referral Services

www.pettravelcenter.com

Here you'll find lists of both national and international accredited veterinarians.

www.shirleys-wellness-cafe.com

This site lists national and international holistic veterinarians and animal wellness consultants.

www.familypetservices.com

Veterinarian information can be found here.

Pet Supplies

The Sherpa Trading Company

www.sherpapet.com

Tails by the Lake, Specialty Shop for Dogs and Cats

www.tailsbythelake.com/bowlsdiners.html.

Wee-Wee Pads

www.weewee.mylanusa.com/

American Pet Foods Overseas

www.petco.com

www.petsmart.com

www.drsfostersmith.com

First-Aid Products

www.medipet.com

www.petfirstaid.org

www.oesl.com
www.healthypet.com
www.1800petmeds.com

Miscellaneous Online Resources

Pet Insurance

www.moneysupermarket.com/petinsurance/
This site offers comparisons of major pet insurers.

Bash Dibra, pet trainer and author

www.bashdibra.com
This author has written numerous books on animal communications and pet training.

www.pawsacrossamerica.com

This Web site campaign promotes responsible pet care and understanding.

Cat Travel Tips

www.associatedcontent.com/article/224566/tips_for_car_travel_with_cats.html

Merck Vet Manual

www.merckvetmanual.com/mvm/index.jsp?cfile=htm/bc/23303.htm

www.petstyle.com

A great source for pet travel information, as well as pet health, lifestyle, and entertainment news, this site also offers a wonderful video library.

Travel Tips for Older Pets

www.srdogs.com

Further Reading

Traveling with Your Pet, 9th Edition: The AAA PetBook, by AAA publishing
   A listing of more than 13,000 pet-friendly, AAA-rated lodgings in the United States and Canada

The Pet Travel and Fun Authority of Best-of-State Places to Stay and Have Fun Along the Way, by M.E. Nelson
   More than 35,000 listings of pet-friendly beaches, parks, accommodations, kennels, shelters, theme parks, and more

Globetrotting Pets: An International Travel Guide, by David Forsythe
   Advice and resources for pet-friendly international travel

Living a Dog's Life: Jazzy, Juicy, and Me, by Cindy Adam
   A great book by one of my dear friends, about her travels with her best friends

The Canine Hiker's Bible, by Doug Gelbert
   Everything you need to know about hiking with your best friend, plus a listing of 225 US pet-friendly parks and national lands (and their regulations)

The Merck/Merial Manual for Pet Health, by Cynthia M. Kahn, Scott Line, eds.
   A great, all-purpose manual for any pet owner

All about my traveling companion

Name_____

Breed/Type of Animal_____

Sex_____

Birthdate_____

Weight_____

Distinguishing Marks_____

Allergies_____

Disabilities/Illnesses _____

_____

Medications_____

Vaccinations (type and date)_____

_____

Veterinarian Contact Information_____

_____

no pet left behind resources

my traveling companion
(paste a photo here)

checklists

What to pack

- [ ] Pet-Preparedness Kit (see page 80)
- [ ] Loss-Prevention Kit (see page 19)
- [ ] First-aid kit (see pages 26, 92)
- [ ] Medications
- [ ] Vaccination papers, health records
- [ ] Travel-appropriate carrier
- [ ] Carrier liners
- [ ] Leash / Harness (don't forget a spare!)
- [ ] Blankets / beds
- [ ] Sweater or coat (if traveling to a cold climate)
- [ ] Food and water bowls
- [ ] Travel-friendly toys (see page 35)
- [ ] Food (and a can opener, if your pet likes canned food)
- [ ] Bottled or frozen water
- [ ] Litter box, litter, and scoop; pooper-scooper or plastic bags
- [ ] Wee-wee pads
- [ ] Stain remover / cleaning supplies

Things to do before traveling

When booking airline tickets

☐ Inform the airline that you are traveling with a pet, and ask for regulation information and under-the-seat dimensions to determine whether your pet will travel cargo or in cabin.

When booking accommodations

☐ Ask hotel for regulations and daycare accommodations for your pet

☐ Make reservations at pet day care/spa (if you are going on a day trip without them)

At least 7 months prior to travel

☐ If traveling internationally, start the application process for obtaining a PETS certificate

☐ Contact embassies for pet travel regulations for your destination

☐ Research your destination to find out what certificates or documents are needed

At least 3 months prior to travel

☐ Register your pet for microchip ID or tags / update microchip or tag identification information

☐ Enroll your pet in obedience classes; start training them for crate travel

1 month prior to travel

☐ Make an appointment with your vet for a checkup, vaccinations, and to obtain all travel certificates needed

☐ Research veterinarians near your travel destination; keep their information with your pet's carrier and in your luggage

2 weeks prior to travel

☐ Recheck with your airline to make sure regulations have not changed

1 week prior to travel

☐ Make / update your Pet-Preparedness Kit (see page 80):
Refill / update all medications
Refresh water and food
Update medical records and certificates

☐ Make a Loss-Prevention Kit (see page 19)

☐ Have your pet groomed; if traveling with a bird, have their wings clipped (see page 85)

☐ Label your pet's crate (see page 22)

☐ Make up "Lost Pet" signs—just in case!—and keep in your luggage

1 night prior to travel

☐ Freeze water in your pet's carrier bowl (if the pet is traveling cargo)

☐ Clip your pet's nails (so they don't break if your pet scratches the inside of her carrier)

The day of travel

☐ Equip the crate with liners, blankets, dry food, and water

☐ 4 hours before check-in, feed your pet a light meal

☐ Exercise your pet before putting them in the carrier

Acknowledgments

In any endeavor it takes a village, as they say, and this book is no different. There are many people to whom I owe a great debt of gratitude for bringing this project to life.

At LifeTime Media, my eternal thanks go to president Jacqueline Grace, who always believed in this project, and executive editor Karyn Gerhard for her tireless work in getting this book put together. Many thanks also to Roger Gorman and Judy McGuire at Reiner Design for the wonderfully charming design. At Thomas Nelson, my thanks go to editor Emily Prather for all of her efforts and to vice president Pamela Clements, for publishing such a handsome work.

But it is no exaggeration to say that, without my mother, Sherpa, SuNae, and all of the wonderful customers that want to travel with their pets, this would not have been possible. Onward and upward!

index

A

air travel
  airport terminals, 13, 53, 96
  birds, 97, 117
  crate labeling, 19, 22, 42, 45, 97
  domestic, 94-97, 176
  etiquette, 53-56
  international, 104, 105-8, 176
  lost pets, 158
  pet insurance, 161, 203
  Pet-Preparedness Kit, 80-81, 211
  soft-sided carrier options, 8, 24-25, 28
  toys, 35, 117
  tranquilizers, 94, 107-8
  travel checklist, 210-11
  ventilation for carriers, 55
  See also health certificates; Loss-
    prevention kit
airline requirements
  approved signs and forms, 22
  birds and cold-blooded pets, 96-97
  carrier size, 13, 28-29, 38, 54
  domestic travel, 94-97, 176
  food and water bowls, 22, 24, 107
  international travel, 104, 105-8, 176
  internet information, 104, 176
  pet behavior, 38, 45
  pet-friendly, 8, 13, 27, 54, 164-75
airport terminals, 13, 53, 96
amphibians. *See* cold-blooded pets
antibiotic creams, 92, 93
anxious pets. *See* fearful pets
automobile travel. *See* car travel

B

babies, 26, 56, 82, 97
  See also kittens; puppies
baby-food, 49, 68
baggage hold. *See* cargo hold travel

Bahamas, 120-21
barking. *See* etiquette; obedience training
beaches
  pet-friendly, 140-41, 146-47, 149, 150
  preparation for, 141, 149
  travel information on, 176, 204
bedding and blankets
  for babies, 26
  car supplies, 77
  car travel acceptance, 38
  chilled pets, 65
  elderly pets, 44
  keeping clean, 24, 39, 113
  options for, 24-25, 113
  Pet-Preparedness Kit, 80
behavior, pet. *See* etiquette; obedience
  training
bike rides, 136
birds
  air travel, 97, 117
  airlines allowing, 164-75
  cage travel, acceptance of, 38, 84
  Canada, travel to and from, 113-15, 117
  car travel, 82, 84, 90
  clipping wings of, 85, 117, 211
  food for, 49, 82, 90, 117
  grooming, 88
  illness, 26, 90, 92
  leashes and harnesses for, 12, 77, 84
  loss-prevention, 155-56
  Mexico, travel to and from, 118, 120
  pet lodgings, 127
  Pet-Preparedness Kit, 80, 81
  senior, 44
  soiling, 39, 84
  toys for, 35, 76, 117
blankets. *See* bedding and blankets
boat rides
  charters, 140, 145, 180-81

dogs, 141-42, 145
ferries, 102, 146, 199-200
international, 111, 145, 199-200
loss-prevention, 155
sunscreen, 149
Boston, 148-49, 182-83
burrs, 131
bus travel, 27, 84-85, 102

C

cabin air travel
  airlines allowing, 164-75
  birds and cold-blooded pets, 96-97
  cargo, compared to, 54-55, 56, 94-96
  etiquette, 53-54
  soft-sided carrier options, 8, 24-25, 28
cages. *See entries under carrier*
camping
  pet ID tags, 21
  pet-friendly campgrounds, 129, 131, 136
  preparation for, 91
  swimming, 132
camps, dog, 57, 127, 131-32, 177-79, 182
Canada, 112-14, 117-18, 198
Cape Cod, 149
car travel
  birds and cold-blooded pets, 77, 82, 84, 90
  carrier acceptance training, 26, 33, 35, 36, 38
  carrier and pet placement, 36, 70, 82
  carrier and restraint options, 24-25, 77, 79, 82
  dog walking areas, 12-13, 50-51, 90, 126
  Eurotunnel, 111-12, 200
  exercise breaks, 61, 66, 90
  fast-food restaurants, 50-51, 62, 75, 126, 134
  first-aid remedies, 92-93

interstate travel, 19, 93-94, 120
leaving pets in cars, 63, 65, 77
long trips, 85, 88-90
Pet-Preparedness Kit, 62, 80-81, 88, 211
popularity of, 27, 88
short trips, 75, 76-79
See also motion sickness
cargo hold travel
  cabin travel, compared to, 54-55, 56, 94-96
  carrier size requirements, 28-29, 38, 54
  carrier ventilation requirements, 55
  crate labeling, 19, 22, 42, 45, 97
  lost pets, 158
  travel checklist, 210, 211
  water and food bowls, 22, 24, 107
  water supply, 54, 106-7, 108
  See also Loss-prevention kit
Caribbean, 120-21
carrier acceptance training, 26, 33, 35, 36, 38-40
carrier liners, 24-25, 39, 113
carrier size
  airline requirements, 13, 28-29, 38, 54
  birds, 84
  cats, 28, 39-40
  dogs, 28-29
carriers, hard-sided. *See* crates, hard-sided
carriers, soft-sided
  air travel options, 8, 24-25, 28
  airline size requirements, 13, 28-29, 38, 54
  car, placement in, 36
  car travel options, 77, 79
  considerations for choosing, 26
  Loss-prevention kit, attachment of, 19
carriers as sun protection, 149

carriers for birds and cold-blooded pets
  air travel, 97, 117
  car travel, 82, 84
  keeping clean, 39, 84
  loss-prevention, 155-56
  pet comfort in, 38, 84
cats
  air travel, 54, 56, 107, 108
  airlines allowing, 164-75
  baby-food, 49
  Canada, travel to, 113
  car travel, 61-62, 66, 77, 80, 90
  carrier, putting into, 36
  carrier options, 8, 24-25, 77, 79
  carrier sizing, 28, 39-40
  carrier training, 38-39
  elderly, 42, 44
  Europe, travel in, 101-2, 108, 110, 111
  hotels, 44, 53, 57, 126
  illness, remedies for, 92, 93
  internet sites, 203
  motion sickness, 26, 68, 90, 92
  Pet-Preparedness Kit, 80, 81
  toys, 35, 53, 76
  travel acceptance, 12, 61, 66
  See also kittens
checklists for travel, 209-11
chewing gum, 131
chilled pets, caring for, 65
city travel
  Boston, 148-49, 182-83
  city parks, 135, 146, 148
  Key West, 149-50, 183-84
  New York City, 146, 148, 176, 184-86
  San Francisco, 134, 146, 176, 186-88
  taxis and subways, 84-85, 148
  Telluride, Colorado, 150, 188
cold-blooded pets
  air travel, 22, 96-97

Canada, travel to, 114-15
car travel, 77, 82
crate travel, 38, 39
elderly, 44
food for, 26, 49, 82
grooming, 88
loss-prevention, 155-56
Pet-Preparedness Kit, 80, 81
travel companionship, 12
collars. See identification, pet; leashes
  and harnesses
condos, 120, 132, 182
constipation, 92
crate labeling
  attachment tips, 19
  exotic and cold-blooded pets, 22, 97
  special-needs pets, 42, 45
  See also Loss-prevention kit
crate training, 26, 33, 35, 36, 38-40
crate-door security, 55, 97
crates, hard-sided
  car, placement in, 36, 79
  considerations for choosing, 26, 79
  food and water bowls, 22, 24, 107
  Loss-prevention kit, attachment of, 19-20
  size requirements for airlines, 28-29,
  38, 54
  USDA ventilation requirements, 55
  See also cargo hold travel; carriers,
  soft-sided
cuts and scrapes, 92, 93

D
diarrhea, 68-69, 92
difficult pets, 38, 45, 61, 88
  See also special-needs pets
dining out. See restaurants
dog camps, 57, 127, 131-32, 177-79, 182
dog parks

metropolitan, 135, 146, 148
roadside rest areas, 13, 50, 90
dog walking
   airport terminals, 13, 53
   city parks, 135, 146, 148
   etiquette, 49-51, 53, 61-62, 90, 150
   fast-food restaurants, 50-51
   motels, 126
   roadside rest areas, 12-13, 50, 90
   walking tours, 140
dogs
   air travel, 22, 53-56, 94
   airport terminals, 13, 53
   boat rides, 141-42, 145
   camping etiquette, 91
   Canada, travel to, 112-13
   car travel, 77, 79, 88
   carrier sizes, 28-29
   crate training, 26, 33, 35, 36, 38-40
   elderly, 42, 44
   Europe, travel in, 101-2, 105, 108, 110
   food for, 49, 76
   grooming, 88, 144
   illness, 26, 51, 68, 90, 92-93
   lakes, 141-44
   Mexico, travel to and from, 118
   Pet-Preparedness Kit, 80, 81
   restaurant etiquette, 135
   restaurants friendly to, 132, 134, 148-49
   therapy certifications, 41, 131
   toys, 35, 56, 76, 135
   walking etiquette, 49-51, 53, 61-62,
   90, 150
   See also beaches; obedience training;
   puppies
domestic air travel, 96-97, 176
driving. See car travel

E

eating out. See restaurants
elderly pets, 42, 44-45, 56, 203
embassies, 190-96
emergencies. See first-aid; Pet
Emergency Preparedness Kit
etiquette
   air travel, 53-56
   beaches, 141, 149
   boats, 142, 145
   camping, 91
   crate cleaning, 39-40
   difficult pets, 45
   Europe, 105
   hotels, 44, 53, 56-57, 125-26
   mountain areas, 144
   parks, 135, 136
   restaurants, 135
   walking dogs, 49-51, 53, 61-62, 90, 150
   See also obedience training
EU. See European Union (EU)
Europe
   boat and train travel, 101-2, 105, 111,
   199-200
   health facilities, 104
   internet information, 112, 198, 199
   microchips, 101, 109, 201
   pet customs, 105
   pet food, 102, 104, 202
   PETS Certificate, 108-11, 112, 210
European Union (EU)
   Form EU 998, 106, 198, 199
   microchips, 201
   PETS Certificate, 110, 111
Eurotunnel, 111-12, 200
exercise
   cats, 53, 61-62, 66, 90
   medical concerns, 51, 63
   motion sickness, aid for, 66

(exercise cont.)
  noise control, aid for, 39, 62-63
  See also dog parks; dog walking
exotic pets
  air travel, 88, 94
  airlines allowing, 164-75
  cage cleaning, 39
  Canada, travel to, 114-15
  crate labeling, 22, 97
  See also birds; cold-blooded pets

F

fearful pets
  car travel, 38, 66
  Pet-Preparedness Kit, 62
  separation anxiety, 26, 45
  socializing, 42, 61
ferrets
  airlines allowing, 168
  Canada, travel to, 114-15
  crate travel, 38, 39
  Europe, travel to, 110, 111
  interstate travel, 94
  Mexico, travel to and from, 120
  pet lodgings, 127
  Pet-Preparedness Kit, 80
  socializing, 61
first-aid
  car travel, 92-93
  hypothermia and chill, 26, 65, 142
  outdoors, 138-39
  overheating, 26, 63
  Pet-Preparedness Kit, 62, 80-81,
    88, 211
  supplies for, 202-3
  See also medical conditions and
    concerns; motion sickness
fish, 93, 164-75
fishing, 142

food, pet
  air travel, schedule for, 106-7
  baby-food, 49, 68
  birds, 49, 82, 90, 117
  bowls fastened to crate, 22, 24, 107
  cold-blooded pets, 26, 49, 82
  dogs, 49, 76
  elderly pets, 44
  Europe, 102, 104, 202
  feeding routines, 61, 102
  instructions attached to crate, 20,
    22, 107
  Pet-Preparedness Kit, 81, 211
  See also motion sickness

G

government regulations. See health
  certificates
grooming, 81, 88, 131, 144, 211
guinea pigs. See rodents

H

hairballs, 92
Hamptons, The, 146
hamsters. See rodents
harnesses. See leashes and harnesses
health care. See first-aid; medical
  conditions and concerns
health certificates
  agency contact information, 19, 112,
    197-99
  air travel in cold temperatures, 106-7
  Bahamas, 121
  boat charters, 145
  cabin air travel, 56
  campgrounds, 131
  Canada, 112-15, 117-18, 198
  countries without health certificates,
    105-6

crate, attached to, 19, 42, 94, 107
European Union, 106, 198, 199
interstate travel, 19, 93-94, 120
Mexico, 118, 120
non-European Union countries, 111
parks, 140
PETS Certificate, 108-11, 112, 210
Puerto Rico, 121
travel checklist, 210-11
United States, bird importation into, 115, 117, 118, 120
hiking, 136, 140, 149, 177
hotels and motels
    etiquette, 44, 53, 56-57, 125-26
    internet information, 176
    pet hotels, 127, 182
    pet ID tags, 21, 129
    pet-friendly, 12, 90, 125-26
    travel checklist, 210
    window signs, 24
    See also city travel; condos; resorts and spas
house-breaking for crates, 39
hypothermia, 26, 65, 142

I
ice, 54, 69
identification, crate. See crate labeling
identification, pet
    foreign travel, 101, 109, 201
    hotels, 21, 129
    loss-prevention, 155, 158
    permanent, 20-21
    travel checklist, 210
    unique ID tags, 21-22
    See also Loss-prevention kit
iguanas. See cold-blooded pets
illness. See first-aid; medical conditions and concerns

insect bites and stings, 92, 138
insurance for pets, 160-61
international air travel, 104, 105-8, 176
international travel checklist, 210-11
international travel information, 176, 190-96
interstate travel, 19, 93-94, 120
island vacations, 120-21
itch relief, 92

K
kennels. See carriers, soft-sided; crates, hard-sided
Key West, 149-50, 183-84
kittens
    air travel, 56, 97, 106
    airlines allowing, 167, 170
    Canada, travel to, 113
    car travel, 82
    travel acceptance, 12, 26, 66

L
labeling, crate. See crate labeling
lakes, 141-44
large dogs
    aging, 42
    air travel, 22, 94
    car travel, 79, 88
    carrier sizing, 29
    diarrhea remedies, 68, 92
    subways, restrictions on, 85
    See also cargo hold travel; crates, hard-sided
leashes and harnesses
    airport security checkpoints, 54
    beaches, 141, 149
    birds, 12, 77, 84
    campgrounds, 91
    car harnesses and barriers, 79, 82

(leashes and harnesses cont.)
    car safety, 76
    cats, 61-62, 66, 77
    city travel, 135, 146, 148
    Europe, 102
    loss-prevention, 155, 156
    mountain areas, 144
    parks, 135, 136
    pet identification, 20, 21, 24, 129, 155
    Pet-Preparedness Kit, 80
    privately controlled areas, 140
    restaurants, 135
    Sherpa Bags, 8, 25
    short car trips, 79, 82
    training, 40-41
    travel preparation, 24, 27, 77, 80
lizards. See cold-blooded pets
Loss-prevention kit
    contents of, 19-20
    crate labeling, 19, 22, 42
    feeding and watering instructions, 20,
    22, 107
    purchasing forms for, 22
    sample form, 206-7
    special-needs pets, 20, 42, 94, 107
    travel checklist, 211
    See also Pet Emergency Preparedness Kit
loss-prevention training, 155-56
lost pets
    finding, 156-58, 160, 201
    flyers, 158-60, 211
lost-and-found pet services, 160, 201

M
medical certificates. See health
    certificates
medical conditions and concerns
    cargo hold travel, 55, 56, 94
    daily health checks, 69

diarrhea, 68-69, 92
elderly pets, 44-45
Europe, treatment in, 104
exercise, 51, 63
hypothermia, 26, 65, 142
internet information, 203
in Loss-prevention kit, 20, 42,
    94, 107
overheating, 26, 63
pet identification tags, 22
Pet-Preparedness Kit, 80, 211
sunburn, 141, 149
tranquilizers, 69, 90, 94, 107-8
veterinarian referral services, 202
water supply, 27, 44, 61, 102
    See also first-aid; motion sickness
Mexico, 118-20
microchips
    benefits of, 20-21
    foreign travel, 101, 109, 201
    loss-prevention, 155, 158
    travel checklist, 210
mineral oil, 92
motels, 12, 90, 126
    See also hotels
motion sickness
    food as aid for, 26, 68-69, 76, 92
    tranquilizers for, 69, 107-8
    warning signs, 66
    withholding food, 61, 68, 90
    withholding water, 68, 69, 107
mountains, 144, 150

N
national parks and forests, 91, 135-36,
    140, 176-77, 204
New York City, 146, 148, 176, 184-86
non-European Union countries, 111

no pet left behind index

O

obedience training
  aggressive pets, 45
  basic commands, 40-41
  beaches, 141
  car travel, 76
  dog camps, 131
  European customs, 105
  loss-prevention, 156
  noise control, 38, 45, 62-63
  restaurants, 135
  therapy dogs, 41, 131
  turning around in carrier, 38-39
  See also etiquette
ocean travel, 111, 145, 199-200
older pets, 42, 44-45, 56, 203
outdoors, first-aid for, 138-39
overheated pets, caring for, 26, 63

P

packing checklist, 209
parks, city, 135, 146, 148
parks, dog. *See* dog parks
parks, national and state, 91, 135-36, 140, 176-77, 204
parrots
  Canada, 113-14
  clipping wings of, 85, 117, 211
  elderly, 44
  Mexico and interstate travel, 120
  motion sickness, 26, 90, 92
  toys, 35, 76, 117
  travel companionship, 12
  See also birds
passenger cabin air travel. *See* cabin air travel
pet carriers. *See* carriers, soft-sided; crates, hard-sided
pet hotels, 127, 182

  See also dog camps
pet insurance, 160-61, 203
pet measurements, 28-29
Pet Emergency Preparedness Kit, 62, 80-81, 88, 211
pet taxis, 85
Pet Travel Scheme (PETS), 108-11, 112, 199-200, 210
pet-therapy classes, 41, 131
poison oak and ivy, 139
poisoning, 92
poop scooping. *See* etiquette
potty training, 39
Puerto Rico, 121
puppies
  air travel, 54, 56, 97, 106
  airlines allowing, 167, 170
  Canada, travel to, 112
  car travel, 80, 82
  public parks, 135
  travel, acceptance of, 26, 39

R

rabbits, 44, 61, 114-15, 117-18, 164-75
rabies vaccinations. *See* health certificates
rail travel. *See* train travel
rats. *See* rodents
reading suggestions, 204
recovery services, 160, 201
  See also lost pets
regulations. *See* health certificates
rental lodgings, 120, 132, 182
reptiles. *See* cold-blooded pets
resorts and spas, 127, 129, 142, 144
restaurants
  car travel, 50-51, 62, 75, 126, 134
  etiquette, 135
  Europe, 105

(restaurants cont.)
   internet information, 176
   pet-friendly, 132, 134, 148-49
road travel. *See* car travel
rodents
   airlines allowing, 164-75
   Canada, travel to, 114-15
   crate travel, 38, 39
   elderly, 44
   loss-prevention, 155-56
   motion sickness, 26
   pet lodgings, 127
   toys, 35
RVing, 24, 129, 131

S

San Francisco, 134, 146, 176, 186-88
scrapes and cuts, 92, 93
sea travel, 111, 145, 199-200
senior pets, 42, 44-45, 56, 203
separation anxiety, 26, 45
Sherpa Bag carriers and totes, 8, 19,
   24-25, 28
Sherpa carrier liners, 113
Sherpa leashes and collars, 8, 25
Sherpa seat covers and throws, 25
Sherpa Trading Company origins, 6-9
Sherpa Trading Company website, 104,
   202
sick pets. *See* first-aid; medical
   conditions and concerns
signs, window, 24
size, carrier. *See* carrier size
skunks, 139
small dogs, 28-29, 42, 68, 92
   See also cabin air travel; carriers,
   soft-sided
snakebites, 138-39
snakes. *See* cold-blooded pets

spas and resorts, 127, 129, 142, 144
special-needs pets
   carrier considerations, 26
   difficult pets, 38, 45, 61, 88
   elderly pets, 42, 44-45, 56, 203
   Loss-prevention kit, 20, 42, 94, 107
   See also fearful pets; medical
   conditions and concerns
state parks, 136, 140, 176-77
stress. *See* fearful pets
subways and taxis, 84-85, 148
sunscreen, 141, 149
swimming, 50, 56, 129, 132
   See also beaches; lakes

T

tags. *See* identification, pet; Loss-
   prevention kit
tar, 131
tattoos, pet, 20
taxis and subways, 84-85, 148
Telluride, Colorado, 150, 188
therapy dogs, 41, 131
ticks, treatment for, 139
time-shares and condos, 120, 132, 182
toilet-training, 39
totes, 24-25, 28-29
tours, 140, 149-50, 176
toys
   air travel, 35, 117
   car travel, 35, 76
   hotels, 53, 56
   Pet-Preparedness Kit, 81
   restaurants, 135
train travel
   Europe, 101-2, 105, 111, 200
   internet information, 200
   tours, 140
   United States, 27, 84

training
  car travel, 38, 66, 75, 76-77
  crate training, 26, 33, 35, 36, 38-40
  loss-prevention, 155-56
  noisy pets, 38, 45, 62-63
  resources on, 203
  toilet-training, 39
  See also obedience training
tranquilizers, 69, 90, 94, 107-8
treats. *See* food, pet

V

veterinarians. *See* health certificates;
  medical conditions and concerns
vomiting, 68, 92

W

water bowls, 22, 24, 82, 107, 108
water supply
  birds and cold-blooded pets, 82, 117
  boat rides, 142
  cargo hold travel, 54, 106-7, 108
  exercising, 51
  for grooming, 88
  instructions attached to crate, 20,
    22, 107
  motion sickness, withholding for, 68,
    69, 107
  Pet-Preparedness Kit, 81, 211
water from home, 27, 44, 61, 102
wilderness areas, 136, 140

About the Authors

Gayle Martz, an award-winning entrepreneur, is best known for creating The Original Sherpa Bag®, the first soft-sided pet carrier endorsed by major airlines. Ms. Martz began her professional life, however, as a flight attendant. During a two-decade career, she received many industry honors, including TWA's Award of Excellence. In 1989, wanting to travel with her Lhasa Apso, Ms. Martz designed a carry-on bag that fit under an airline seat, thus enabling her dog to travel in the passenger cabin. Ms. Martz then proceeded to single-handedly persuade airlines to change their policies and permit small pets to travel alongside their owners. Her pioneering efforts captured the attention of press nationwide, and, in 1996, she won the prestigious Women of Enterprise Award from Avon Products Inc. and the U.S. Small Business Administration. Today, The Sherpa Pet Trading Company® manufactures more than a dozen styles of travel bags and accessories that are sold worldwide. Through her company Ms. Martz continues to pursue her mission of increasing awareness of safe pet travel and improving the lives of animal lovers and their pets.

Delilah Smittle is a full-time editor and writer who specializes in the subjects of pets, home, and hobbies. She has written about pets for the magazine *Pets, Part of the Family,* and Reader's Digest books, and has contributed to or edited more than two dozen books, including *The Backyard Beekeeper, The Backyard Birdwatcher, Reader's Digest's Homemade,* and *Rodale's Complete Garden Problem Solver.* Delilah has at one time or another shared her life with pet birds, fish, amphibians, reptiles, cats, and dogs. She now writes and lives in semi-rural eastern Pennsylvania, where she shares her house with a Boston terrier named Duke, and her backyard with a retired chicken named Grizz, ducks, goldfish ponds, and a wealth of wildlife.